The Spiritual Quest of Francis Wagstaffe

About the editors

Toby Forward was born in Coventry in 1950. He has worked in a variety of jobs: as a waiter, warehouse man, at a holiday camp, petrol pump attendant, teacher and clergyman. He is now a full-time writer and lives in Beverley, Yorkshire with his wife and two daughters. Toby is a versatile author who reaches a wide audience of young children, teenagers and adults. His books include *The Toad Lady, Travelling Backwards* and *Wyvern Winter* (all published by *Puffin Books*).

The Rev'd David Johnson was educated at Dame Allan's School, Newcastle upon Tyne, and Selwyn College, Cambridge, where he read Divinity. He was President of The Union in 1976. After a wait of two years at Cuddesdon Theological College he was ordained to a title in London. In 1982 he was co-author of the best-selling *Not The Church Times* and was subsequently TV critic of the real thing for four years. He is now a rural pluralist, and, when not in demand as an after-dinner speaker, lives quietly with his dogs in the Northamptonshire countryside. In 1984 he was awarded the Cross of St. Rombaut (2nd Class) for meritorious service to the Belgian Roman Catholic Church.

The Spiritual Quest of
Francis Wagstaffe

Edited by Toby Forward & David Johnson

First published in 1994
by GRACEWING
Fowler Wright Books
Southern Avenue, Leominster
Herefordshire HR6 0QF

Gracewing Books are distributed

in New Zealand by

Catholic Supplies Ltd
180 Adelaide Road
Wellington 1
New Zealand

in Australia by

Charles Paine Pty
8 Ferris Street
North Parramatta
NSW 2151 Australia

in U.S.A. by

Morehouse Publishing
P.O. Box 1321
Harrisburg
PA 17105 U.S.A.

in Canada by

Meakin & Associates
Unit 17, 18 Auriga Drive
Nepean, Ontario
KZE 7Y5 Canada

A royalty from the sale of this book will be paid to
St. Peter's Young Homeless Support Centre, Leicester.

Cover design and interior illustration by John Ryan
Typesetting by Stephanie Hollis
Printed by The Cromwell Press, Melksham, Wiltshire

ISBN 0 85244 298 X

Preface

I must confess that I was somewhat taken aback to be asked by the publishers to write the preface to this collection of letters. It is common knowledge in the East Riding that a certain *froideur* exists between ourselves in the Old Kalendrist Church, and the Old Northern Catholick Church of the East Riding. I am surprised to hear that news of this rift has not penetrated to the West Midlands, but there you are. At any rate, the contract is signed now, and my cheque is in the bank, so I feel free to be honest and open about some matters that the public have the right to know.

I know that there are some who will think that I am taking advantage of Francis Wagstaffe's discomfiture and ill-fortune in writing this preface. I can only say that I feel that the hand of providence has intervened, giving me the opportunity. Life in a Police Cell in Tangiers must be uncomfortable enough without losing control of your memoirs. I am told that he expects to be freed at any time, with all charges dropped, but I remain skeptical. An informant, who keeps an eye on the Old Northern Catholicks for us, watched Kevin depart on his mercy mission to Tangiers, from Hull Docks, and if that young man thinks that the quickest way to North Africa is to sign on as a steward on a Tramp Steamer to Bangkok, then he's got another thing coming. He should have learned a bit of geography since the days when he was a barman in the Double M Club.

Quite simply, the Old Northern Catholick Church is a spurious offshoot of our own Body, and Mar Francis is a fraud. His orders, though valid, are highly irregular, and he should be subservient to us, as the Primate of Holderness and Filey. His real authority is about as genuine as the recipe of his Cumberland Sausage, which was the best emetic in the county. It therefore follows that all their property is our fief, and that copyright of these letters is the privilege of the Old Kalendrists.

I share the expectation of the BBC that these letters will prove to be a bestseller. So, I have no hesitation in commending the book to you, Gentle Reader, in the full expectation that our legal experts will wrest the proceeds from the grasp of the East Riding and vest them in us.

Buy early. Buy lots. Give them to your friends for Christmas.

HIS CELESTIAL WHITENESS, MAR TERRY II
PATRIARCH OF THE HUMBER, METROPOLITAN AND PRIMATE
ARCHBISHOP OF SUNK ISLAND
ORDER OF SAINT ELFEDA OF THORNGUMBALD (1st CLASS)

Being the Correspondence of

His Grace
the Most Reverend the Archbishop of the
Old Northern Catholick Church of
the East Riding

Mar Francis II

Metropolitan and Primate,
Knight Grand Commander of the Order of Saint John
of Beverley (lst Class)

Francis Wagstaffe
28 Danesway
Beverley
East Riding
Yorkshire
HU17 7JQ

The Bishop of Leicester,
Bishop's Palace,
Leicester.

21st April 1993

Dear Bishop,

I was dismayed and disgusted to hear your 'Thought for the Day' on Radio Four this morning.

I am not in the least interested in whether or not you can run a marathon, but the activities of the Apostle Paul are of great interest to me and to all believers.

You say that Saint Paul, like you, took part in athletic and gymnastics excercises in ancient Greece. How ridiculous! You must be unaware that the word gymnast comes from the latin word meaning 'naked'! All athletes in the ancient world competed naked. Do you seriously suggest that Saint Paul disported himself in the games area in the nude.

I hope you will take the earliest opportunity to remedy this lapse of taste and biblical scholarship, to an audience on national radio, not just a small note at the bottom of your next newsletter to the diocese, alongside the Mothers Union notes and the list of newly unfrocked clergy!

Yours sincerely,

Francis Wagstaffe

BISHOP'S LODGE, 10 SPRINGFIELD ROAD, LEICESTER LE2 3BD

Telephone (0533) 708985   Fax (0533) 703288

from The Rt Revd Dr Thomas Butler, The Bishop of Leicester

23rd April 1993

Dear Mr Wagstaff,

Thank you for your letter.

I am sorry that you were dismayed and disgusted by Wednesday's 'Thought for the Day'.

Whilst not quite using such strong language, I was a little disturbed myself when I discovered that only the first minute of my talk was actually broadcast and after that the line between Leicester and London failed. I enclose a copy of the full 'Thought'. This might not change your opinion in the slightest, but it will at least give you the opportunity of reading what I was intending to say.

With best wishes.

Grace and Peace

Thomas Leicester

Mr F Wagstaff
28 Danesway
Beverley
East Riding
HU17 7JQ

BISHOP'S LODGE, 10 SPRINGFIELD ROAD, LEICESTER LE2 3BD

Telephone (0533) 708985   Fax (0533) 703288

from The Rt Revd Dr Thomas Butler, The Bishop of Leicester

Thought for the Day - 21 April 1993

Good Morning. Today my wife and I are still nursing our aching muscles and wearing our medals with pride, having run for The Church Urban Fund and Christians Aware in Sunday's London marathon.

It was quite an event, yet for non-athletes like ourselves it was also somewhat of an ordeal for no amount of training really prepares you for a 26 mile run on hard roads. We were lucky though in having a wealth of advice available during our time of preparation. In particular, Loughborough University is not too far away, and its sporting faculty over the years has trained a host of fine athletes including Sebastian Coe. I spent a valuable morning there whilst the experts put me on the treadmill and took blood samples, and then on the basis of this data gave me helpful advice about training and the pace which I should aim to maintain during the race.

The marathon is based of course on the ancient Greek legend of the run of a soldier from Marathon to Athens to convey the good news of the defeat of the invading Persian army. But although the ancient Greeks were mad about athletics it seems very unlikely that the marathon was part of their sporting calander. The maximum length of race in their stadia was aprroximately three miles - quite long enough for any sane person to want to run.

There's no record of the Apostle Paul actually taking part in these races, but they must have made an impression on him for he writes in one of his letters to the Corintians - At the games as you know all the runners take part, though only one wins the prize. You must also run to win. Every athlete goes into strict training. They do it to win a fading garland; we to win a garland that never fades.

So, the journey of faith, the journey of life is serious, it's no fun-run, it has a significant goal and it's worth investing energy in training and preparation. Of course much of the training has to be undertaken as we go along. We have to strengthen our spiritual, our mental, our moral muscles as best we can, mostly by trial and error.

But neither are we without help. People, such as the Apostle Paul, have run the race before us and have wisdom to offer. The New Testament partly coming from his pen has given meaning and purpose to the lives of people living in very different places at very different times in history. And the same thing can be said of the holy books and traditions of many of the great world religions. They are the spiritual and moral equivalents of Loughborough's sporting training programmes and we're foolish if we don't take advantage of them as we run our race.

Religion offers no instant solution to life's problems, no escape from aches and pains and confusions - but it offers advice, encouragement and hope - the hope that ultimately nothing good or kind or generous in life is wasted for the journey has goodness as its very goal - the garland that never fades. That's

Francis Wagstaffe
28 Danesway
Beverley
East Riding
Yorkshire
HU17 7JQ

The Bishop of Oxford.
Bishop's House,
72 Linton Road,
Oxford
OX2 6UL

23rd February 1993

Dear Bishop,

Forgive me for intruding on your time on a deeply personal matter, but my
nephew Colin who is up at the University overheard at an Oxford
hairdresser's one of the barbers telling a customer that your toupee is of
such quality that few people outside his establishment know of its
existence.

My nephew is very discreet (as am I) and this information only slipped out
late on New Year's Eve at a family party, and the following morning he
resolutely refused to expand on the subject or divulge the name of the
firm.

As a favour to a fellow former Greenjacket I was wondering if you would be
kind enough to favour me with the name and address of your wig-maker. I
would treat this information with the utmost confidence. After all,
neither of us wants to end up looking like the late Eric Morcambe!

Yours gratefully,

Francis Wagstaffe

P.S. I very much enjoyed 'Is there a Gospel for the Rich', which my nephew
Colin passed on to me. That bit about the camel's eye always seemed to me
to be an obvoius early misprint.

THE DIOCESE OF OXFORD

BERKSHIRE · BUCKINGHAMSHIRE · OXFORDSHIRE

FROM THE BISHOP OF OXFORD
The Right Reverend Richard Harries

8 March 1993

Dear Francis,

Thank you for your letter. I am sorry to disappoint you, however,
but my hair is in fact my own! What strange rumours get around.

I wish you luck in your search for an adequate toupee.

With all good wishes.

Yours sincerely,

F. Wagstaffe, Esq.,
28 Danesway,
Beverley,
East Riding,
Yorks HU17 7JQ

Diocesan Church House, North Hinksey, Oxford OX2 0NB
Tel: Oxford (0865) 244566   Fax: Oxford (0865) 790470

Francis Wagstaffe
28 Danesway
Beverley
East Riding
Yorkshire
HU17 7JQ

The Bishop of Oxford.
Diocesan Church House,
North Hinksey,
Oxford
OX2 ONB

10 April 1993

Dear Bishop,

I must say I'm disappointed in your letter to me. I know it's
a bit embarrassing to have to wear a toupee, and not the sort
of thing you like to get around, but I did promise you
absolute discretion. May I appeal to you once more to cast
aside your feelings and help out a fellow sufferer? Perhaps I
laid it on a bit thick last time, when I said your wig was
undetectable. Of course, Colin, who has seen you in action,
says it's very good, but that it is clearly not your own hair
(to the trained eye). I'm sorry to be so blunt, but I do think
you could hlep me. I appreciate that you don't want to be
known as the Terry Wogan of the C of E, but my lips are
sealed.

Do you keep it on with double-sided tape, or some sort of
spirit gum? It must be tricky when you have to keep on putting
your bishop's hat on and taking it off in church!

I know you will help me. Look into your heart - doesn't
Christian charity come above personal vanity? I'm going to be
in Oxford in May, to visit Colin. I might be able to pop in
and see you, just on the off chance.

Yours sincerely,

Francis Wagstaffe

Francis Wagstaffe

Flat C, 81 Camberwell Church Street. LONDON SE5 8RB

The Bishop of Hull,
Hullen House.
Woodfield Lane.
Hessle.
Hull.
HU13 0ES

22nd March 1993

Dear Bishop,

Forgive me for trespassing on your time, but Stabber o' Riley says he knew you in the navy and that you are a good sort. He also dug out your address for me, from a book in the library.

The thing is I have a small house in Gloucestershire, where I spend a lot of time, and we have a Mayday Dwarf Hurling Competition. I'm on the Committee. It's a fund raising event for charity. I can't tell you where it is, for reasons which will become obvious!

We always open procedings with a short service led by the Vicar. Sadly, our parson died last year, and he didn't leave us a form of service. The new man has refused point blank to have anything to do with the event. Not the best start to his new job. Between you and me, I think there was something funny about the way he was appointed. He isn't a married man, if you get my drift.

I can promise you that it's all good fun, and the dwarves love it as much as anyone. These left-wing parsons make me mad.

Stabber says that you were always reckonned to be a shortarse (forgive the service slang. I bet it takes you back a bit!) These days they call it vertically challenged, don't they? So, could you let me have some Bible passages and a prayer or two that I can read out at the start of the event? I'd rather a proper parson did it, but we're not going to be beaten. My nephew, Colin says there's a bit in the Old Testament about dwarves. I've never been able to find it, and the last person said he was getting confused with something else, but he wouldn't explain what. Do you know where it is?

Stabber sends best wishes. He says do you remember that exotic dancer at the New Years Eve Party? The one who hid a bottle of Guinness! He says he's still got the bottle and he's never opened it. He won't tell me how he got it off her!

Hoping you can help us.

Yours sincerely,

Francis Wagstaffe

9

Francis Wagstaffe

Flat C, 81 Camberwell Church Street. LONDON SE5 8RB

The Bishop of Hull,
Hullen House.
Woodfield Lane.
Hessle.
Hull.
HU13 0ES

3rd April 1993

Dear Bishop,

I wonder if you've got that service ready for the Mayday Dwarf
Hurling yet? Can you get it to me ASAP?

I've got another favour to ask as well. I wouldn't ask, but as
I said, Stabber o' Riley says you're a sport, so here goes.

One of our dwarves has come up lucky with free air tickets
from Hoover, but he's got to take the flight toot sweet. So
he's going to be away in the U S of A for the last week of
April and first week of May. That leaves us a dwarf short! Do
you think you could step into the breach? We would make sure
you were hurled by our best man, and you land in a specially
designed reception pit (fully padded, so there are no
bruises). It is all quite safe, good fun, and raises a lot of
money for charity. What do you say? We could probably get you
on the local news. Who knows, it might even give you a leg up
the greasy pole of promotion. We're looking for a new bishop
here, so if you made a good impression with the locals it
could go in your favour. You are a family man aren't you? I
tried to get Ladbroke's to take a bet that the new Bishop here
would be married with squads of children but they weren't
interested. Pity, it's a sure fire bet.

Hoping you can come. We'd put you up for the night with Mrs
Potter, who's a widow and a good sort!

Yours,

Francis Wagstaffe

Flat C, 81 Camberwell Church Street. LONDON SE5 8RB

The Bishop of Hull,
Hullen House.
Woodfield Lane.
Hessle.
Hull.
HU13 OES

26th April 1993

Dear Bishop,

I'm a bit worried you haven't been getting my letters. Stabber
o' Riley says his wife once nobbled his secretary and got her
to extract all the golfing invitations (and anything else that
looked like a bit of fun) out of his post. Stabber wondered
why everyone had cut him dead till he found out. Then it was
skates on for girlie and advertise for a new one. And you
don't need me to tell you what fun he had then.

Anyway, Stabber thinks your secretary might be up to the same
sort of thing because you haven't answered yet. To tell you
the truth, the whole thing's been a bit of a pig's pudding —
what with the parson refusing to do the prayers, our best
dwarf going on holiday, and now we've had to postpone because
the Squire says we can't use his land for hurling on Mayday on
account of its being a socialist holiday. He's all for these
new plans for rerouting the festivities to Nelson's birthday.
Anyway, the upshot is, we can have the hurling on his land on
May 31st, Spring Bank Holiday, because he reckons that's got
no associations with the Reds. It's probably Rosa Luxemburg's
birthday or something half-arsed like that — still, not many
Spartacists in our part of Gloucester so the silly fool won't
get wind of that!

What Stabber sugests is that we make a foray up to your neck
of the woods in the first week of May, put up at a guest house
somewhere and look you up. That way, your secretary won't be
able to stop you having a meeting. We'll try to bring Mrs
Potter with us, so you can have a look at her! I'll bring the
video of last year's dwarf hurling so you can see it's
perfectly safe.

See you in May.

Yours,

Francis Wagstaffe
28 Danesway
Beverley
East Riding
Yorkshire
HU17 7JQ

The Bishop of Winchester
Bishop's Palace
Winchester.

29th January 1993

Dear Bishop,

Stabber o' Reilly tells me he saw you at his borther-in-law's Lodge the
other day, so, as a fellow member of the Craft, and a Provincial Offical,
would you use your contacts to get me two tickets for the Royal Enclosure
at Ascot this year (Ladies' Day if possible, I'd like to take Mrs Wagstaffe
on a day when she can get full value out of the hat).

I thought you lot weren't supposed to belong any more, but don't worry, I
won't breathe a word off the Square. I know how news travels. But I take
it it would be all right if I told our Provincial Officers to include you
on the list of Chaplains in the North?

May the Great Architect protect you.

Yours fraternally,

Francis Wagstaffe
28 Danesway
Beverley
East Riding
Yorkshire
HU17 7JQ

The Bishop of Winchester
Bishop's Palace
Winchester.

10th March 199s

Dear Bishop,

I don't want to seem a pest, but could you let me know what's hapenned about those tickets for Royal Ascot that you promised me. I don't need the actual tickets straight away, but I do need to know which day they're for?

I've looked up your qualifications for our Handbook. The girl in the library was holpeless. They all are these days, aren't they? Anyway, with a bit of prompting from Yours Truly she got herself organised in the end, and this is what we've come up with for your entry.

HONORARY CHAPLAIN IN THE NORTHERN PROVINCE

The Right Rev Colin Clement Walter James. born. 1926 Kings College Cambridge (third class. History) Lord Bishop of Winchester.

It can go straight in like that, or if you want, I can add your own Lodge number and any Provincial Honours and titles you hold. Just let me know.

Yours Fraternally,

Francis Wagstaffe

Francis Wagstaffe
28 Danesway
Beverley
East Riding
Yorkshire
HU17 7JQ

The Bishop of Winchester's Secretary
Bishop's Palace
Winchester.

27th March 1993

Dear Sir or Madam,

Could you please let me have a list of the times and places where the
Bishop will be confirming in April and May? I enclose a stamped addressed
envelope.

Thank you.

Yours faithfully,

Francis Wagstaffe

From the Bishop of Winchester
(0962) 854050

Wolvesey,
Winchester,
SO23 9ND

2 April 1993

Dear Mr. Wagstaffe,

Thank you for your letter of 27 March asking about Confirmation Services this month and next. It is not the Bishop's custom to circulate lists of his appointments, but if you have a relative or friend due to be Confirmed by him do please let me know.

I am conscious that you have written to the Bishop on two occasions earlier this year. No discourtesy was meant in that you have not received replies; the Bishop was, however, baffled by your reference to Royal Ascot tickets, which are quite outside his jurisdiction!

With all good wishes,

Yours sincerely,

C.V. Peterson
Lay Assistant

Francis Wagstaffe, Esq.,
28 Danesway,
Beverley,
East Riding,
Yorkshire HU17 7JQ.

Francis Wagstaffe
28 Danesway
Beverley
East Riding
Yorkshire
HU17 7JQ

The Bishop of Winchester,
Wolvesey,
Winchester.
SO23 9ND

11th April 1993

Dear Bishop,

I have a very serious matter to report to you.

I wrote to you on the 29th January and the 10th March, but
received no reply. This made me smell a rat. You are not a man
to ignore a civil letter, especially a fraternal one! So, I
set a trap. I wrote to your secretary, asking for your
confirmation dates for April and May. This is a simple
document, freely available, I guess. But it was refused me,
even though I had paid for its postage. Now I know that you
are not receiving your post. It is being monitored and
filtered by someone who calls himself C.V. Peterson.

C.V. Peterson makes the ludicrous claim that the dates and
times when you confirm are a secret! Do you let the people who
are being confirmed know? Or do you drive them to a secret
destination, blindfold, in a sealed van? Come off it,
Peterson! Your bishop and I are On the Square, even if you're
not, and we know what's what.

Then, this stooge, Peterson, says that you had my earlier
letters but did not answer because you were baffled by them!
You, Sir, are not a man to be baffled by a request for a race
ticket! Have you ever been to Royal Ascot yourself? How did
you get your tickets, might I ask? I know you would help out a
chap making a brotherly request. And even if you couldn't
help, you'd at least reply. Peterson knows what a discourtesy
it is to ignore a letter, but we've caught him out.

Now, Bishop. I enclose another SAE. I have no doubt that Mr
so-called Peterson will let you send me a confirmation list,
and that you will sign it in your own hand, to prove that he
has not filtered this letter out.

I am very sorry to have to bring this to your attention, but
I've seen Yes, Minister, and I know how you people in high
office are given the run-around by lackeys! Keeping you in the
dark.

The printers have got the copy for the Yearbook, and it will
be going to press in the next couple of weeks. I'll send you a
copy as soon as I have one.

Yours fraternally,

Francis Wagstaffe

Francis Wagstaffe

28 Danesway, Beverley, East Riding, Yorkshire. HU17 7JQ

The Bishop of Winchester,
Wolvesey,
Winchester.
SO23 9ND

27th April 1993

Dear Bishop,

I don't suppose your man Peterson will let you see this
letter, but at least I can feel secure that I will be able to
have a word with you and tip you off about the way he is
treating your post.

Stabber o' Reilly managed to lay his hands on one of your
secret lists and we'll be coming to see you ASAP. I hope to
make it on the 2nd May, but if not, will certainly be able to
get down by either the 28th or 30th. It all depends on how Mrs
Wagstaffe feels and whether I can get the Alvis to start. I
always moth ball her for the winter (the Alvis, not Mrs
Wagstaffe), and I can't always get her going in the Spring
(Mrs Wagstaffe, not the Alvis).
You'll recognise me easily enough. I'll be the middle-aged man
in spectacles with a dark suit and patterned tie. It will be a
privilage to hear you preach and to share a fraternal
handshake!

Yours fraternally,

Francis Wagstaffe

From the Bishop of Winchester
(0962) 854050

Wolvesey,
Winchester,
SO23 9ND

23 April 1993

Dear Mr Wagstaffe,

This fellow Peterson (admirable and good hearted chap, though he is) is now on leave, and your letter of 11th April has reached me. Indeed I have discovered a hoard of good things emanating from your address about 2 feet 6 inches down (we have not gone metric here) in one of his pending trays. (Oddly enough his In and Out trays are coated in dust, indicating years of dis-use).

You ask about tickets for Ascot; but alas, like the psalmist, 'I do not exercise myself in great matters that are too high for me'. I have no influence in that arena. Have you thought of approaching some one in the racing world? Perhaps one of the gentlemen presiding over the affairs at Aintree could help.

However, there is the risk which no doubt you and Mrs Wagstaffe are weighing anxiously, that should there be similar difficulties and disappointments in getting the Ascot competitors past the starting line let alone the finishing line, then the racing world, and the great British television public, would be denied the sight of Mrs Wagstaffe's hat. (Incidentally, is it fully insured against possible molestation from Animal Rights enthusiasts?)

My advice is to abandon the long and dangerous trip to Ascot and have a healthy hike, or hitch an economical lift to York, and enjoy the Ebor handicap. Who knows, on a fine day you might even be lucky enough to secure the Archbishop's autograph; he and the handicap enjoy the same signature.

Yours sincerely,

Colin Winton:

Francis Wagstaffe Esq.,
27 Danesway,
Beverley,
East Riding,
Yorkshire,
HU17 7JQ

Francis Wagstaffe
28 Danesway
Beverley
East Riding
Yorkshire
HU17 7JQ

The Bishop of Sodor and Man,
Bishop's House,
Quarterbridge Road.
Douglas.
I. O. M.

24th April 1993

Dear Bishop,

I hope you do not mind if I trespass on your time, but I have
a proposal which might be of benefit to us both.

A few years ago, I was obliged to sell what was universally
acknowledged to be the best Prep School in the East Riding of
Yorkshire - Potter Hall. I am sure you are aware that there is
a lot of jealousy in the world of independent education, and
nasty rumors get around. Still that's water under the bridge
now. I was lucky, in that I was able to sell the premises at
the height of the property boom. The dust has now settled and
due to wise investment I am in a position to start up again. I
particularly want to set up on the island because of its wise
policy on corporal punishment in schools - a discipline I
find essential to good order.

There are three things I wonder if you could help me with.

Is there a parish on the island which is finding it difficult
to support a clergyman? I could offer half a stipend to
someone who would be our Chaplain and do a bit of Scripture.

Do you know of any property near to such a parish which would
be suitable for a school of about two hundred boys?

What is the present position with regard to the European Court
of Human Rights vis a vis *le vice*? I would want to bring some
of my best staff with me and some of them are naturally
nervous about working in a restrictive atmosphere. I would
like to able to set their minds at rest.

I am going to be in Douglas in the second week of May, looking
around for a property. I'll call in on you for further
discussions.

Yours faithfully,

Francis Wagstaffe

The Lord Bishop of Sodor & Man

Bishop's House
Quarterbridge Road
Douglas
Isle of Man
Telephone: 0624-622108
Facsimile: 0624-672890

29 April 1993

Mr Francis Wagstaffe
28 Danesway
Beverley
East Riding
YORKSHIRE HU17 7JQ

Dear Mr. Wagstaffe.

Thank you for your letter of 24 April 1993.

You will be aware that the Island already has a Prep School in Castletown and in a small country the field is limited. Similarly there is a very conservative atmosphere to moral issues, even though Legislation here has been changed in recent months.

One property which would be ideal both for current building and future extension is The Nunnery in Douglas, which is currently the home of Mr Robert Sangster. I understand that it is on the market.

Yours sincerely

+Noël Sodor and Man.

Bishop

ACORN PRESS

28 Danesway, Beverley, East Riding, Yorkshire.

The Bishop of Chelmsford.
Bishopscourt,
Margaretting,
Ingatestone.
Essex

22nd March 1993

Dear Bishop,

We are a small, independent local publishing house. We have had great success with books on local interest and are planning to expend into new fields. We still intend to base our marketing on local interest, but we are spreading our net into new regions.

Our research has shown us that there would be good sales in Essex for a book of Essex Girl jokes. These have been very popular recently. There would be no actual author, as the jokes are in the public domain, as it were, and have been collected by a researcher who is a full-time member of our staff, so no royalties would be paid in that department.

Local books always sell better if a local celebrity contributes to them. We wondered if you would like to write a short Preface, say 500 words, to our book, as the Bishop concerned with Essex? We could offer you a fee of £50.00p immediately, against a royalty of 50p per copy, selling at a cover price of £5.00p. The sales would be brisk, I can promise you, and we could supply you with an 'author pack' for you to sell yourself. I expect you do a lot of after-dinner speaking - Masonics, Rugby Clubs, that sort of thing. You could use a couple of the jokes in your talk, and then mention that the book is on sale at the back of the hall.

We have censored the jokes, keeping away from the rather risque variety, but allowing some licence for what we like to think of as music hall or seaside postcard humour. Here are a couple of examples.

Q: What does an Essex girl use for protection when she's having sex?

A: A bus shelter.

Q: What's the difference between an Essex girl and a Kit Kat?

Francis Wagstaffe & Partners

A: You only get four fingers in a Kit Kat.

Q: What's the difference between a walrus and an Essex girl?

A: One's got a moustache and smells of fish. The other one's a walrus.

I hope you can join with us on this enterprise. It would show that the Church knows what's going on in the world and could do no end of good.

Yours faithfully,

Francis Wagstaffe

ACORN PRESS

28 Danesway, Beverley, East Riding, Yorkshire.

The Bishop of Chelmsford,
Bishopscourt,
Margaretting,
Ingatestone.
Essex

7th April 1993

Dear Bishop,

I'm going to be in Essex from the 29th April to the 2nd May,
inclusive, with a photographer, getting some snaps for the
book. Can you have your preface ready by then? I'll call in
and pick it up, and we can get some publicity photos of you at
the same time. Any particular day? Or shall I just take pot
luck?

Yours sincerely,

Francis Wagstaffe

THE BISHOP OF CHELMSFORD'S CHAPLAIN
THE REVEREND PHILIP NEED
Tel: 0277 352001
Fax: 0277 355374

BISHOPSCOURT
MARGARETTING
INGATESTONE
ESSEX CM4 0HD

F. Wagstaffe Esq.,
Acorn Press,
28 Danesway,
Beverley,
Humberside.

21st April, 1993.

Dear Mr. Wagstaffe,

Following your recent communications with the Bishop of Chelmsford concerning your book, I write to say that it will not be possible for the Bishop to be involved in any way with this project.

The Bishop is concerned to afford women their rightful place in society today and cannot be associated with anything which would appear to demean them. I have to say that there would be no point in your coming to Bishopscourt next week.

Yours sincerely,

Philip Need

Francis Wagstaffe
28 Danesway
Beverley
East Riding
Yorkshire
HU17 7JQ

The Bishop of Salisbury
The Palace
Salisbury
Wilts

22nd February 1993

Dear Bishop,

Like you, I didn't have much of an education, and I've always been
interested in you since my nephew Colin told me you'd been made Bishop of
Salisbury. I'm always glad when an old boy of my own college (the
University of Life) gets on against the odds. Anyway, you'll see why I'm
writing to help you now.
I've cast your horoscope for the coming year. You'll be delighted to know
that there's nothing very bad in it, but there are one or two dicey dates
for you. The thing is, you should on no account travel on the following
dates –

February 28th (short notice I know)
March 10th
April 12th
June 4th
August 12th
December 25th. I don't suppose you go far that day anyway!

Can you check them against your diary.

I've got other dates for you to do with money, love, meetings, and how to
influence people to do what they don't want to do. I'm going to be in
Salisbury in March, so I'll call on you and give you the full chart and the
list of dates. Are there any other matters you want me to include in it –
(ways to hurt an enemy, how to win on the pools, that sort of thing) Let me
know and I'll consult the stars before I come. Is there any parking near
by you? I've got a bad hip and can't walk far.

Good Fortune!

Francis Wagstaffe

THE BISHOP OF SALISBURY'S OFFICE
SOUTH CANONRY
71 THE CLOSE,
SALISBURY SP1 2ER

Telephone: Salisbury (0722) 334031
Fax No: (0722) 413112

24 February 1993

Dear Mr Wagstaffe

The Bishop has received your letter of 22 February.

We note that you are in the Salisbury area next month, but unfortunately, we have to tell you that the official diary is very full and we are sorry we are unable to add anything further at present.

Yours sincerely

(Secretary)

Francis Wagstaffe Esq
28 Danesway
Beverley
East Riding
HU17 7JQ

Francis Wagstaffe
28 Danesway
Beverley
East Riding
Yorkshire
HU17 7JQ

The Bishop of Salisbury
The Bishop of Salisbury's Offices.
South Canonry.
71 The Close.
Salisbury.
SP1 2ER

10th March 1993

Dear Bishop,

I'm a bit worried that you haven't had my letter. I wrote to
you about your horoscope, which has taken me a long time to
prepare, and I've had a short note back from a girl who claims
to be your secretary. I can't tell you what her name is
because I can't read her writing.

The thing is, I know how difficult it is to get reliable
staff, so I thought she might have taken it on herself to
answer without showing you the letter. These girls just out of
school have'nt got any nowse and it seemed to me to be very
rude of her not to have let you know what I was writing about.

I know you wouldn't ignore me just because I haven't got a row
of letters after my name. After all you're the same. Do you
think they might be taking advantage of you because you don't
know the ropes? My nephew Colin says that sort of thing often
happens. He says the Pope hardly knows what's going on in the
church and that he's a prisoner of something called the
cordial, which is all the cardinals.

What I've done is. I've put off my trip to Salisbury until
after I've heard from you when it would be a good time to
call.

Colin also says he thinks your girl might think I was trying
to get money out of you. Nothing could be further from the
truth. I would offer you the full horoscope free of charge, as
a gift to the church.

I may as well tell you, though I wasn't going to mention it
till we met, that I've done one for the Archbishop of
Canterbury, and it's very bad news for him. He's going to go
through a really bad time, just at the same time as you find
yourself promoted to a VERY HIGH OFFICE. Obviously the stars
can't be more precise than that, but anyone can read between
the lines can't they. The details of the dates of this are in
the full horoscope which I'll show you. Between you and me,

I'll be glad to see him go. Colin says his spectacles do more
damage to the Church of England than any number of bishops
caught making themselves a disgrace with trainee monks! Hard
words, but I think you'll agree he has a point.

Looking forward to seeing you.

Good Fortune!

Francis Wagstaffe

THE BISHOP OF SALISBURY
Bishop John A. Baker

SOUTH CANONRY
71 THE CLOSE
SALISBURY SP1 2ER

Telephone: Salisbury (0722) 334031
Fax No: (0722) 413112

12 March 1993

Dear Mr Wagstaffe

Thank you for your warm and charming letter of 10 March.

Let me assure you that I do see all correspondence addressed to me. My postbag is not as large as the Pope's, and my senior secretary who replied to you on my instructions is a valued colleague of great experience without whom I really would be in a mess!

So any discourtesy was entirely mine, and I do apologise.

The reason why I did not write myself is that I did not wish to say anything that might cause you distress to no purpose. But now I obviously ought to make it clear that as a Christian I can give no countenance whatever to astrology. The New Testament makes it clear that even if the heavenly bodies once had power over our lives they do so no longer. Christ has delivered us from that bondage as from others. Whatever happens to me God can guide and support me through it, and bring me at the last to eternal life, and no one and nothing else can do that.

By the way I ought to add that I think Dr Carey is one of the best things that has happened to the Church of England in a long time. No doubt he will have heavy crosses to bear, but that is what true servants of Jesus have to expect. His bishops will give him loyal backing, I am sure, though I myself will have to be less active in doing so, as I am due to retire in the Autumn.

With warm good wishes (but not for your astrology!)

Yours sincerely,
+ John Sarum

Francis Wagstaffe Esq
28 Danesway
Beverley
East Riding
Yorkshire
HU17 7JQ

Francis Wagstaffe
28 Danesway
Beverley
East Riding
Yorkshire
HU17 7JQ

The Bishop of Salisbury
The Bishop of Salisbury's Offices.
South Canonry.
71 The Close.
Salisbury.
SP1 2ER

31st March 1993

Dear Bishop,

I seem ot have put my foot in it with you, so I am sorry.
Please give my apologies to the girl who does your post for
you. I did not mean to upset her. I am sure she does a good
job.

I must say your letter was a bit of a winder. I did not think
that you would be a doubter about the Art of Astrology. It
took the wind out of my sails all right. But I've been looking
through it and I am interested to see that you do not actually
doubt astrology itself, but that you are toeing the party line
about it. I wish you had more freedom to say what you think in
public, but it was good of you to tip me the wink in private.

You say, 'the heavenly bodies once had power over our lives'.
Of course they did! And so they must still have. I see what
you are driving at. You are not allowed to look into what
their influence on us will be. But I can do it for you, can't
I? I understand that the Church stops you being an astrologer
yourself through its rules and regulations, but it doesn't
stop you being guided by me, does it? Especially as you admit
the influence of the heavens.

I could slip you the chart in private if you want. When are
you going to be doing a confirmation in April? Let me know and
I'll come. I'll be very discreet about it.

By the way, I am sorry that you have been forced into early
retirement by the Archbishop of Canterbury. My nephew Colin
says that you were once a promising man. Never mind, he will
spoil a few other careers before he's done, but his chart is
very bad! And I've looked at yours again, added some new
calculations, and you're definitely going places! Can you tell
me the exact place where you were born, and the time of day?
That helps to make a more detailed chart.

Yours sincerely,

Francis Wagstaffe

Francis Wagstaffe
28 Danesway
Beverley
East Riding
Yorkshire
HU17 7JQ

The Bishop of Durham,
Bishop's Palace.
Durham.

29th March 1993

Deer Bishup,

I expect yu no that George Bernard Shaw left muni in hiz wil for the reform
ov speling and the introdukshun ov a standud simpul methud. So far, nowon
haz clamed this muni. I am miself dislexic and so I hav an intrest in
wurking for a betur sistum ov speling.

Wot I want to do iz to set up a grupe ov wel-conectid pepl hoo wil giv ther
names az paytruns ov a susyity for a nyu way ov speling. I am riting to
meny leeding dislexics, including yorself and Mikul Heselteen and Soosn
Hamshur.

I can ashoor yu that if we cun get enuf intrest in this projek then we wil
do a lot ov gud and wil find no shortig ov funds from the istate of George
Bernard Shaw.

I hope yu can help by giving yor name az a paytron. It wil give hope to
such a lot ov pelp if a prominunt pursun like yu gets involvd. Do yu think
yu can intres a church publishur in publishing Bibuls and prare buks in our
nu sistum? I no there iz a need.

Thank yu.

Yos sicseerly,

Francis Wagstaffe

FROM THE BISHOP OF DURHAM
THE RIGHT REVEREND
D. E. JENKINS

AUCKLAND CASTLE,
BISHOP AUCKLAND,
CO. DURHAM,
DL14 7NR.
BISHOP AUCKLAND 602576

The Diocese
of Durham

Francis Wagstaffe
28 Danesway
Beverley
East Riding
Yorkshire HU17 7JQ

7 April 1993

Dear Francis Wagstaffe

Thank you for your letter to the Bishop dated 29 March. He has asked me to respond on his behalf, as he has so many commitments there is an average 6 to 8 week delay before he is able to get round to responding personally to non-diocesan.

The Bishop is not personally dislexic. In the case of your project he very much regrets he does not have the time to take up another initiative, however important the cause.

With many regrets

Yours sincerely

Glennis Henderson

For the Bishop's Office

Francis Wagstaffe
28 Danesway
Beverley
East Riding
Yorkshire
HU17 7JQ

The Bishop of Durham,
Aukland Castle,
Bishop Aukland
Co. Durham.
DL14 7NR

10th April 1993

Deer Bishup,

I am sori to hav had yor anser to mi last letur. It iz sined 'Glennis
Henderson', but I beleev that that iz just a fols naim yu ar using and that
yu rote it yorself, panefuly and with grate efurt. Luk at the evidens. The
secund sentens is compleetly rong in its gramer, with a confushun abowt
wich is the mane verb, 'repond' in the furst harf, or 'is' aftur the
commer. And ther iz and a funi use ov the expreshun 'responding personally
to non-diocesan'. This iz not a letur bi a purson hoo nose how to rite the
inglish langwig. Az if that wos not enuf, yu hav spelt 'dislexic' in mi nu
sistum, not 'dyslexic' as eny ordinuri pursn wud. So, I hav cort yu owt! Mi
nefu Colin furst put me on to yor problem. He haz hurd yu on the telly and
red abowt yu in the papurs and he ses it iz kwyt cleer yu hav nevur red the
Bibul.

I wish yu wud admit yu ar dislexic(!). Yu wur probly teesd at skul besors
yu wer not brite. But I no that dislexic pepl can be brite. Yu can cast
awai yor shaim and let pepl no yor problm. It wud help them and it wud fre
yu from yor feelins ov inadikwusi. Yu wud be abul to rede the Bibul and orl
sorts ov things.

I am gowing to be in the north eest sune. Abowt the end of Aprul or the
staat of Ma. I wil corl in on yu and tri to perswade yu to help yorself and
othurs. Wot dait iz best for yu? Or shal I just taik pott luk.

Yors sinseerly,

Francis Wagstaffe

FROM THE BISHOP OF DURHAM
THE RIGHT REVEREND
D. E. JENKINS

AUCKLAND CASTLE,
BISHOP AUCKLAND,
CO. DURHAM,
DL14 7NR.
BISHOP AUCKLAND 602576

The Diocese
of Durham

Mr F Wagstaffe
28 Danesway
Beverley
East Riding
Yorkshire HU17 7JQ

16 April 1993

Dear Mr Wagstaffe

I have received your letter of 10 April. You appear to be so disturbed by your dyslexia that you feel free to be abusive and ungracious - not least about members of my staff.

I can assure that you will get no help from me in any campaign which is conducted in such a manner. Nor will you receive any further communications from this office.

Yours sincerely

Francis Wagstaffe
28 Danesway
Beverley
East Riding
Yorkshire
HU17 7JQ

The Bishop of Durham,
Aukland Castle,
Bishop Aukland
Co. Durham.
DL14 7NR

21st April 1993

Deer Bishup,

I am sori to hav had yor anser to mi last letur. I reely du not no wot I
can hav sed that yu think iz abusiv or or ungrashus. Pleez wud yu aksept my
sinseer apolojiz. Wotevur I did rong woz kwyt unintenshunul. I hoap yu wil
find it in yor hart to undurstand and tu forgiv!

But I am afrade that I stil hav a mishun to the pore disleksick pepl ov
this cuntry. Can I for the last tyme beg yu to admit to yor handycap and
help owr corz. Plees!

I am sori that I hav to beg in this way, and that I hav onli yor oan leturs
az pruf ov yor problum, but if yu luk at yor last letur yu wil sea that yu
hav ritn 'I can assure that you will get no help...' a norml inglish ritur
wud hav put 'I can assure you that you will get no help...' And wen yu sine
yor naim yu du not spel Durham rite. So yu sea, yu nede help. We can giv it
tu yu. Mi nu speling sistem wud fre yu from yor problum.

I no yu ar a clevur man and that if yu cud cum to turms with yor problum yu
wud abul to du so mutch gud - tu yorself az wel az tu uthurs.

I incloas a bocks ov chokluts for yor staf to sher owt az a sine ov mi soro
and apolojiz if I ofendid thum. I am sori that ther ar no orinj cremes but
I gaiv thum to Mrs Wagstaffe. We ar penshunurs and canot aford chocks usuly
and thi orinj cremes ar hur favrit.

Az I sed in mi last letur, I wil be in the north eest at the staat ov mai.
I wil corl in to sea yu and maik amends on thi thurd forth fifth or sickth
of Mai. Let mi no if won ov thees iz betur for yu than anuthur. If I do not
heer from yu I wil no that yu don't mind wich dai I cum.

With sinceer apolojiz and hoaps that yu wil forgiv me.

Yours evur,

Francis Wagstaffe

FROM THE BISHOP OF DURHAM
THE RIGHT REVEREND
D. E. JENKINS

AUCKLAND CASTLE,
BISHOP AUCKLAND,
CO. DURHAM,
DL14 7NR.
BISHOP AUCKLAND 602576

The Diocese
of Durham

Mr F Wagstaffe
28 Danesway
Beverley
East Riding
Yorkshire HU17 7JQ

23 April 1993

Dear Mr Wagstaffe

Thank you for your letter of 21 April received in the Bishop's Office today, together with the box of chocolates which you kindly sent as a token of your apologies.

Whilst I appreciate the gesture, I would feel happier if the chocolates were given to Mrs Wagstaffe, and hope you accept the return of these in good faith.

In respect of the penultimate paragraph of your letter, I would inform you that the Bishop is out of the country during the first week in May and it would be fruitless, therefore, for you to call in to see him.

As previously stated, he simply does not have the time to take on any further commitments or causes outside of the diocese and cannot, therefore, enter into any further correspondence with you.

Yours sincerely

Glennis Henderson (Mrs)
Secretary within The Bishop of Durham's Office

Francis Wagstaffe
28 Danesway
Beverley
East Riding
Yorkshire
HU17 7JQ

The Bishop of Carlisle,
Bishop's Palace.
Carlisle.

26th March 1993

Dear Bishop,

I recently retired from my business as a pork butcher in
Beverley. I expect you'll have heard of us. We are, or were,
famous for our Cumberland sausages. I'd still be in the
business now if I hadn't had an arthritic hip. Anyway, with no
children I sold the shop on, but I kept the recipe for the
sausages. I want to stress that straight away to show you that
there is no business interest in my proposal.

What I want to do is to pay for a tribute in stone to be
erected in your cathedral as the home of the Cumberland
sausage. It would be tasteful and well done, nothing shoddy,
but it would have to have a true and faithful representatoin
of the Cumberland sausage on it.

It would be good for your trade, bringing some trippers in,
and you could put a fridge in the cathedral shop and sell
sausages. I have read about the financial problems the church
is in and this would help out. I am sorry to have to say that
I could not let you have the recipe for my own sausages, as I
want that to die with me. We would put it in a lead casket and
wall it up in the monument. Then, when people came to take
snaps and things, they could look up and see a bit of
butcher's magic and mystery and ponder on the secret recipe.

I am going to be having a bit of a holiday in the Lakes in
May, before the tourists ruin it. We could look at some
designs for the stone then. What date would suit you?

Yours sincerely,

Francis Wagstaffe

38

The Bishop of Carlisle

The Right Reverend Ian Harland, Rose Castle, Dalston, Carlisle CA5 7BZ

Telephone 069 96 274 Fax 069 96 550

Date: 7.4.93

SUBJECT: . . CATHEDRAL . STONE . . . .

This is to acknowledge with thanks safe receipt of your letter of 26.3.93.

Yours sincerely

J Boyd (Mrs)
Personal Secretary

Francis Wagstaffe
28 Danesway
Beverley
East Riding
Yorkshire
HU17 7JQ

The Bishop of Carlisle,
Rose Castle.
Dalston.
Carlisle.
CA5 7BZ

23rd April 1993

Dear Bishop,

Thank you for your letter of the 7th April approving my scheme
for a momument to the Cumberland Sausage in your cathedral.
Following your approval, I have had designs for the stone
drawn up by Mr. F Elwell, of Beverley. He is a good man and
did the designs for my shop front and meat store. He is not
cheap, but he is quality. He has done three designs for you to
chose from, all featuring the sausage and a scriptural text.

As I said, I am going to be in the Lakes in the first week of
May, and can call in with the drawings. What date would suit
you best? Or should I just take pot luck? I have found Dalston
on my map.

Yours sincerely

Francis Wagstaffe

The Bishop of Carlisle
The Right Reverend Ian Harland, Rose Castle, Dalston, Carlisle CA5 7BZ
Telephone 06974 76274 Fax 06974 76550

29 April 1993

Mr F Wagstaffe
Beverley
Yorks

Dear Mr Wagstaffe

CARLISLE CATHEDRAL

I am writing to you in response to your letters of 26 March and 23 April 1993, concerning which there seems to have been some misunderstanding.

There is no question of my having approved your scheme for a monument in Carlisle Cathedral. My letter of 7 April 1993 to which you refer can only have been an acknowledgement of your first letter from my Secretary.

Any monuments proposed for the Cathedral are entirely the responsibility of the Dean and Chapter who are guided by advisory committees who have very exacting requirements and standards which have to be met. As Bishop, I have absolutely no say in the matter. I am sorry that this was not made clear to you earlier, but I had no idea that you were intending so early to start thinking in terms of designs.

Your letters have been forward to the Dean with whom all future correspondence should be conducted.

All good wishes.

Yours sincerely

+Ian Carlisl:

cc The Dean

Francis Wagstaffe
28 Danesway
Beverley
East Riding
Yorkshire
HU17 7JQ

The Bishop of Bath and Wells,
Bishop's Palace.
Wells.
Somerset.

26th April 1993

Dear Bishop,

My nephew, Colin, has had the good fortune to be left a beach
hut in Weston-Super-Mare by his late aunt (not my wife).
Colin, although not rich, is comfortably situated, and he
wishes to put his inheritance to some use which would serve
others. We have discussed this and have agreed that the best
thing would be for us to open it during the summer months as
what Colin calls an oratory (for beach missions, I imagine).
Could you give us some advice about how this would be opened?
Is there a special service, and would you be prepared to take
it? Also, how ought it to be furnished? I favour a simple
style, with a small library of religious books, a portable
pulpit and a tea urn. Colin prefers something more elaborate,
with an altar, a series of lamps and provision for 'reserving
the blessed sacrament' (I hope I quote him correctly.) Could
you please settle which it ought to be?

Colin and I are going to make a foray into the West Country in
the first week of May, to inspect the premises. We will call
in on you if that would help, to show you the plans we have
made. Would any particular day of the week suit you better, or
shall we try pot luck?

Thank you for your help.

Yours sincerely,

Francis Wagstaffe

THE BISHOP OF BATH AND WELLS
The Right Reverend James Thompson

The Palace   Wells   Somerset   BA5 2PD   Telephone Wells (0749) 672341   Fax (0749) 679355

From The Reverend Prebendary Geoffrey Marlow
Bishop's Chaplain and Pastoral Assistant

Mr. Francis Wagstaffe,
28 Danesway,
Beverley,
East Riding, Yorkshire HU17 7JQ   7 May 1993

Dear Mr. Wagstaffe,

The Bishop has asked me to thank you for your recent letter and to reply on his behalf.   How very kind of your nephew to want to use his beach-hut in the service of the Church.   I think the way forward would be to discover which parish it is in so that the Vicar could be involved in the discussions.   Perhaps you could let me know and we can then move the discussion on from there.   I look forward to hearing from you again.
With every good wish.

                    Yours sincerely,

                    Geoffrey Marlow

Francis Wagstaffe
28 Danesway
Beverley
East Riding
Yorkshire
HU17 7JQ

The Bishop of Bristol,
Bishop's House.
Clifton Hill
Bristol

11th March 1993

Dear Bishop,

I hope you do not mind my writing to you, but I was given your
name by our local parson, who seems to think you're the person
I need to appoach. I am writing to you in your capacity as
Chairman of ABM, on a delicate matter.

My nephew, Colin, intends offering himself as a candidate for
ordination. He has reformed himself from being a somewhat
wayward youth into (what I gather from a distance) to be a
settled and industrious young man in the retail sports
clothing industry.

Without entering into his spiritual qualifications and
aptitude to be a parson, which I am not in a position to
judge, there appears to me to be one factor which might
mitigate against him and on which I would like your advice.

When he was much younger he got involved in a rather
'theatrical' set, and a series of unsteady relationships, as a
result of which he ended up with a tattoo on the back of his
left wrist of an anchored heart surmounting the word 'Kevin'.
This is not immediately obvious but it is there beneath his
cuff for anyone to see who is in the know.

Colin's vicar in Brighton laughs this off simply as folie de
jeunesse and says nobody these days would be bothered two
hoots, but it is the sort of thing which is certainly not
acceptable in my part of the world. Perhaps you may think I'm
old fashioned but I think it will count against him at his
selection board, and he ought to have it removed before he
presents himself. What do you think?

Also, do you happen to know if this can be done on the NHS? I
seem to recall reading something about this a few months back
in the Daily Mail

Yours faithfully,

Francis Wagstaffe

THE BISHOP OF BRISTOL
The Right Reverend Barry Rogerson

Bishop's House   •   Clifton Hill   •   Bristol BS8 1BW

Fax: 0272 239670   Tel: 0272 730222

15th March, 1993.

Dear Mr. Wagstaffe,

Thank you very much for your letter of 11th March. I suspect your local parish priest was right in directing your letter to me as Chairman of the Advisory Board of Ministry.

Obviously, the Diocesan Director of Ordinands in the Diocese of Chichester is the person who must deal directly with the issue surrounding your nephew, Colin, as every diocese is an independent unit and it is the responsibility of the Diocesan Bishop to sponsor and to recommend for training after a person has attended a Bishops' Selection Conference.

I am sure that the Selectors are as the Scripture says - 'looking at the heart' rather than at the outward appearance of a candidate. If Colin has a true vocation and has already begun to show the gifts of the Spirit which are necessary for the working out of that vocation then I am sure the issue of a tattoo will not sway the matter.

I have no idea how many people have been recommended for training who have a tattoo of the variety which you describe but I know at least one who has been to a Selection Conference and was recommended for training who sports such a tattoo. But, I am sure, if Colin feels that this is something which is an embarrassment to him then he should talk this over with his Diocesan Director of Ordinands rather than his parish priest and I believe that, in the past, the National Health Service has in fact helped people with this particular problem. I am sure you are aware of the pressures on the National Health Service and the future may not be quite as positive as it has been in the past.

So can I put your mind at rest - I don't believe that the presence of a tattoo is the most important factor but if there are problems then I think Colin should talk to his Diocesan Director of Ordinands.

With best wishes.
Yours sincerely,

+ Barry Bristol;

Mr. F. Wagstaffe,
28 Danesway,
Beverley,
Yorks. HU17 7JQ.

Francis Wagstaffe
28 Danesway
Beverley
East Riding
Yorkshire
HU17 7JQ

The Bishop of Coventry.
Bishop's Palace
Coventry.

22nd February 1992

Dear Bishop,

I'm not a believer myself. Frankly I was put off years ago by the toffee
nosed public schoolboys who all seemed to climb the greasy pole in the
Church of England. But my nephew Colin, who lives in Bradford, where you
used to be the bishop, says that you're a real sort of man. He tells me
that you pulled yourself up by your bootstraps and that your were a runny
nosed urchin with the arse hanging out of your trousers in Northern
Ireland. Good for you! I'm a self-made man as well.
Anyway what I want to say is, that if you could let me know where I can
read about your life story in proper detail I could almost be tempted to be
a believer. I feel sort of immortal yearnings as I get older. I'm also
very impressed with Ian Paisley who's a self made man and a 'Prod' like us
as well. I might as well tell you that Ive got no truck with Catholics,
but you'll be the same as me on that as well. Do you think God could have
been responsible for making Colin tell me about you, it seems a bit too
much of a coincidence that we should be so much like each other doesn't it.
He moves in mysterious way! God I mean not Colin.
I bet you've written a book or two about your early life. What are they
called and where can I buy them.
I want to make some sort of donation to a church fund, to show willing in
my change of heart. I'd prefer it to be one to fight the Pope if possible.
What do you recommend. Or anything really. Name your favourite good
cause.

I'm going to be in Coventry in March, so I'll call in and have a word with
you about how to join up.

All best wishes.

Francis Wagstaffe

The Bishop's House·Davenport Road·Coventry CV5 6PW

From The Bishop of Coventry

Telephone (0203) 672244
Fax No. (0203) 713271

1st March, 1993.

Dear Francis Wagstaffe,

Thanks so much for your letter.

Unfortunately, you got the wrong person!

I would like to claim to be 'a real sort of man' but I do have to
confess that I don't quite have the credentials to that title which your
nephew, Colin, found in the man who was, when he met him, Bishop of Bradford
and who is now in fact not Bishop of Coventry, but Bishop of Southwark.

That man is my good and dear friend, Robert Williamson of 38
Tooting Bec Gardens, London, SW16 1QZ.

I am quite sure that you will get on well with him and that it
would be best if you and he take it from there without my getting in the
way.

I am sorry to miss the opportunity of meeting you, but I'm quite
sure that you ought to get straight through to Bishop Robert whom I know you
will like very much.

I do want to assure you of my prayers and warmest wishes and my
hope that you get as far as London when you come south in March and be able
to go and see Robert then if it's possible!

I've sent your letter straight on to him and I expect he will be
in touch with you!

Warmest wishes,

†Simon Coventry
(Barrington-
Ward)

Mr. Francis Wagstaffe,
28 Danesway,
Beverley,
East Riding,
Yorkshire,
HU17 7JQ.

Francis Wagstaffe
28 Danesway
Beverley
East Riding
Yorkshire
HU17 7JQ

The Bishop of Coventry.
THe Bishop's House.
Davenport Road.
Coventry.
CV5 6PW

10th March 1993

Dear Bishop,

Thnka you for your letter. I'm sorry I made the mistake about who you are.
I don't know how Colin got hold of the sticky end of that smelly stick.

I got the girl on the library to look you up in Whos Who, and it turns out
you went to Eton and Cambridge. Whoops! I hope you'll ignore what I said
about public schoolboys. There's good and bad in everyone I suppose.

Anyway, you seemed a decent sort, passing my letter on to the other chap,
and youre obviously well-connected, so I wondered if you could lay your
hands on a couple of tickets for a Buckingham Palace Garden Party for me?

I'm not a monarchist myself, but Mrs Wagstaffe has got a soft spot for
royalty and she'd love to go. What do you reckon to what theyre getting up
to these days? I think it's a disgrace. Can you tell me the truth about the
Prince of Wales? Can he be King if he's split up?

Sorry about that other mix up. Least said soonest mended.

Yours sincerely,

Francis Wagstaffe

The Bishop's House·Davenport Road·Coventry CV5 6PW

From The Bishop of Coventry

Telephone (0203) 672244
Fax No. (0203) 713271

18th March, 1993.

Dear Francis, if I may,

Thanks for your letter and for letting me off with a caution, in spite of my being so dreadfully establishment.

I fear, however, that even with that misleading air of well-connectedness, I am not able to lay hands on tickets for the Buckingham Palace Garden Party!

I would love to have fixed such a thing for you and Mrs. Wagstaffe if I could have. But unfortunately I don't have that sort of pull! I don't even know how the guests are chosen, except that I have experienced the fact that bishops get invited. If I hear anything from anyone who knows about such things, I'll certainly remember your inquiry and let you know.

I still believe in the Monarchy as a symbol. It does seem to me incredibly sad that the younger generation have so mucked up their marriages, but I suppose in this they're just epitomising what has happened to so many of their contemporaries. It is indeed sad.

As for the Prince of Wales. I think the answer to your question depends on public perception nearer the time. I suppose now that such things are so much more widely accepted than they were, it is just possible that he might still be able to be King without Diana there. But it does seem a tragedy. I keep hoping and praying for a miracle by which they will somehow come back together. I know that is hoping for an awful lot. Nonetheless, in my own experience, stranger things have happened and there have been more astonishing answers to prayer, so who knows?

If not, it might be that they went on to the next generation.

What I think they've really needed is what most of us need at heart, some good spiritual and pastoral counselling and some really good, I mean spiritually and morally good friends. That's the only way of being 'well-connected' that really counts to my mind. If we can be genuinely connected with a few people who are connected to God, it's a great help to any of us.

All the best for your getting to meet Bishop Robert!

Thanks for your very good letter.

Every good wish,

+Simon Coventry

Mr. Francis Wagstaffe,
28 Danesway,
Beverley,
East Riding,
Yorkshire,
HU17 7JQ.

Francis Wagstaffe
28 Danesway
Beverley
East Riding
Yorkshire
HU17 7JQ

The Bishop of Guildford,
Bishop's Palace.
Guildford.
Surrey.

26th March 1993

Dear Bishop,

I have been taking a close interest in Church affairs since I
retired a few years ago, and I was very impressed with your
speech in the General Synod. I spent the whole day watching
the television, glued to my set. You were wonderful. All the
time I was listening to you and admiring the way you played
with the emotions of the house, clouding the issue when you
were on uncertain ground, leading them up blind alleys when
your arguments were weak, and so on, I was aware that I had
seen you somewhere but I could not work out where.

Then, while I was watching the television again this week (you
do get on a lot, don't you!) I saw a film called Circus of
Horrors, and the penny dropped. One of yours! Those were the
days when films were films, not sadistic displays of you-know-
what! I don't think you were calling yourself Anton Diffring
in the synod, but I can't remember what you did use. Is
Diffring your real name and you changed it when you left the
stage, or is the other one your real name and Diffring your
acting nom-de-guerre? When I told my nephew Colin who you were
he said that everyone knew that. He says he read it in a
Church newspaper.

I must say that the write-up for it in the Radio Times made
Circus of Horrors sound like the General Synod! Read this - 'A
bizarre British horror film with Anton Diffring as the plastic
surgeon more professionally interested in female
disfigurement, who runs a circus staring his patients as a
sideline. The excitement Diffring finds in his mutilated girls
is mirrored by the voyeuristic aspect of the circus, which
trades on the grotesque, but the film strays into the realm of
exploitation and wallows in the excesses it purports to
criticise'! A bit near the mark, eh? Isn't it funny the way
life repeats itself?

There is however a more sombre side to my letter. Even though
you acted up a lot on the day in synod, and you were on
slippery ground a lot of the time, the thing is. YOU ARE DEAD
RIGHT! If only they had taken your wise advice and chucked the
Bill out. When the Church of England does ordain women it will
be a grotesque disfigurement. I will leave the Church as soon
as the first woman is ordained. Where should I go? As far as

I'm concerned I'll go wherever you do. But I won't be a Roman
Catholic and kiss the Pope's toe. Give us a lead.

Why don't they use you more on the TV? Old films are one
thing, but we could do with you on live. That Harry Secombe is
useless. You should do that sort of thing with your acting
experience.

Can you send me a signed photograph of yourself? I'd like one
of the one's where you play a German officer, if that's
possible. But anything, really.

Many thanks.

Yours sincerely,

Francis Wagstaffe

From   THE BISHOP OF GUILDFORD
       The Right Reverend Michael Adie
Telephone Guildford (0483) 573922
Fax   Guildford (0483) 32663

WILLOW GRANGE,
WOKING ROAD,
GUILDFORD, SURREY GU4 7QS

15 April 1993

Mr Francis Wagstaffe
28 Danesway
Beverley
East Riding
Yorkshire
HU17 7JQ

Dear Mr Wagstaffe

I am responding to your letter of the 26 March 1993 to Bishop
Michael, in my capacity as his Chaplain and as a parish priest
myself. I was very sorry to read the style and tone of your
letter which seemed to me to be most uncharitable and
unworthy. Nothing is ever helped by this kind of abusive
letter and certainly it does no service to the Gospel.

I have worked closely for a number of years now with
Bishop Michael and know him to be someone who trys to combine
his own search for truth with an ever listening ear to other
views. I hope that perhaps, particularly at this Eastertide
you will reflect again on the appropriate ways in which
Christians and others should relate to each other when their
views differ.

Yours sincerely

The Revd Guy Wilkinson
Bishop's Chaplain

Francis Wagstaffe
28 Danesway
Beverley
East Riding
Yorkshire
HU17 7JQ

The Bishop of Guildford,
Willow Grange,
Woking Road.
Guildford.
Surrey.
GU4 7QS

17th April 1993

Dear Bishop,

I hope you don't mind me writing to you again, but I'm a bit
flummoxed and hope you can help me. I have had a letter from
someone caling himself Guy Wilkinson, who says he is your
chaplain. He accuses me of writing an uncharitable and
unworthy letter to you, and he says that I have been abusive.
I am quite at a loss. I wrote and complimented you on your
speech in the synod. I praised you for the lead you were
giving us in the fight against preistesses, and I said how
much I admired the work you did when you were an actor. I hope
that none of these things is abusive or uncharitable. Let me
repeat, reverend Sir, that I admire all these things in you.

I hope I did not speak out of turn. Perhaps I should not even
write to a bishop. The truth is, I have always admired
theatricals (up to a point, but I'll tell you about that in a
moment), and that I would have liked a picture of you because
I think you are one of our finest actors from a period when
films were something we could be proud of. I suspect you left
the profession because you did not like the turn it was
taking. Let me tell you - neither do I!

As I say, I like theatricals. My late sister, Colin's mother,
was a chambermaid in a theatrical boarding house and I met
many of the stars and found them to be wonderful people. And
here is hte point I mentioned earlier. There are some who do
not uphold the standards of their art and lead girls astray.
Sadly, Colin's mother found herself in an interesting
condition as a result of working amongst theatricals. She has
never divulged the name of the particular player involved, but
my nephew bears a striking resemblance to the late Denis
Price.

I have shown Mr Wilkinson's letter to Colin, and he says he
wonders if you ever authorised such an epistle. He noticed
that Mr Wilkinson writes that you are 'someone who trys to
combine....'. Well! Is that the sentence of an educated man?
Or a clergyman of the Church which boasts the heritage of
Cramner? We think that he intercepted my letter to you and you
have not seen it. I hope so, because that is the only possible
explanation for such a misunderstanding.

If I have offended you in any way, please accept my most
sincere apologies and my continuing regard for you as a fine
actor and a great leader in the church's fight against the
monstrous regiment of women in these difficult days.

If you can let me have one of your old photos I would be very
grateful.

Yours sincerely,

Framin Wagstaffe

Francis Wagstaffe
28 Danesway
Beverley
East Riding
Yorkshire
HU17 7JQ

The Bishop of St Albans.
Abbey Gate House.
St Albans
Herts
AL3 4HD

12th March 1993

Dear Bishop,

I have a shrewd suspicion that this letter will come as no surprise to you. You may even have been waiting to receive it. But I must not leap ahead with my story.

To begin at the beginning. I have for a period of nearly a year now been undergoing a process of regression at the hands of a skilled hypnotherapist. In these sessions I have been made aware of some of my previous lives. No, made aware is not strong enough for what has happened. I have relived them. I have been there again.

In many of these lives I have been an ordinary person, of no importance whatsoever. But, recently, I have been taken back to a time of great disturbance both in the land and in my own heart.

I have for many years now known that I have done a great wrong, but it had been hidden from me. Under hypnosis I experienced a terrible revelation. I was in a huge crowd of people, who were all baying for blood, and I stood on a platform with a row of men with nooses round their necks. At a signal, I tried to hang one of the men, but he leaped from the platform, and hung, still conscious from the rope. In a trice, I followed him, and in the most brutal and bloody fashion I disembowelled him. His hands were tied behind his back, but the look of pity and terror on his face did nothing to stop the me that was that executioner. I can only say that the me who writes this to you now is a different person, purified by many rebirths and that I stand in shame for the wickedness I did. In a terrible moment he fixed me with a stare, and before he fell to screaming in agony, he said 'We shall meet again, master!'

I was as you can understand distraught when I was returned to normal consciousness after this ordeal. I recounted it, not without tears, to my hypnotherapist, who did his best to soothe my conscience. He told me that dreams and fantasies sometimes took the place of reality and that it may not have been a real past life. But I knew from his face that he did not believe this nay more than I do.

I lived with the anxiety of this memory for many months, trying to push it to the back of my mind, but it kept on popping up. Then, led one day by a strange force while I was changing my library boks, I wandered to the New Returns shelf and picked up a book at random. I need not tell you the horror I felt when I opened it and saw. as plain as day, an engraving of the scene I have just described to you! Reading on, it was as I have said. And that the man who I killed was none other than Guy Fawkes!

I showed the book to my hyponotherapist who said that he feared that it was so, and that in his experience such vivid regressions were always true. He also said that they always led to a meeting of the two people in their present lives! Putting me again into a deep trance he led me back to that scaffold. This time, it was dark and lonely, the deed done. I travelled through the years, seeing myself in the lives I had already re-experienced, until I was led, again by a mysterious force, into an Abbey. I wandered round this Abbey, alone and silent, and saw the dark figure of a man in tall pointed hat!

On my return to full consciouness I told the hypontherapist what had happened. He said that the figure in the hat was Guy Fawkes in this life! I could see that he knew something else but would not tell me then. He told me to look at books of Abbeys and see if I could recognise it.

Now you will be aware of what I am coming to! It was St Alban's. I drew the hat for him, and he said it was a bishops miter.

I know from my own experience that you will have been expecting this letter. You too will have had promptings that all was not well with you and that there was someone you needed to meet. I am that man! You are Guy Fawkes! Did you suspect something of the kind?

I feel the burden of my guilt already lifting as I write to you. I know that you will forgive me what I did all those years ago. Say you will! I was an ignorant man, acting under what I believed to be true. Say you forgive me! A word from you would be enough, I think, though I may need to hear it from your own lips. Say when I can come and meet you and we can be reconciled.

In the meantime, do you have a picture of yourself you could send me? With a word for me? I need to see if you still bear the likeness of that poor disembowelled man.

Yours in sorrow and hope,

Francis Wagstaffe

The Bishop of St Albans
Abbey Gate House, St Albans, Hertfordshire AL3 4HD

Tel: 0727 853305
Fax: 0727 846715

30 March 1993

Dear Mr Wagstaffe

Thank you for your letter of 12 March. I am sorry to disappoint you, but I can assure you that it came as a complete surprise! I could only wish that I were able to ease your conscience though I am bound to say that I think you are suffering in a way which is quite unnecessary. Even if I believed in reincarnation, which I do not, I could not see how one should need to bear guilt from one life to another. The Christian faith does recognise our moral responsibility before others and before God, but it is the experience of Christians down the ages that true forgiveness is found through the Cross of Jesus Christ, where God Himself experiences the guilt on our behalf and offers us free forgiveness and reconciliation. And there is surely no more appropriate time to reflect on that than now as we approach Holy Week and Easter. I believe more than I can say that the blood of Christ can cleanse the darkest of consciences.

I am sorry that I am not able to give you the reply that you expected and I do pray that you will find the peace which you are seeking.

Yours sincerely

John St Albans

Francis Wagstaffe Esq
28 Danesway
Beverley
East Riding
Yorkshire
HU17 7JQ

Francis Wagstaffe
28 Danesway
Beverley
East Riding
Yorkshire
HU17 7JQ

The Bishop of St Albans.
Abbey Gate House.
St Albans
Herts
AL3 4HD

3rd April 1993

Dear Bishop,

Your letter has thrown me into a state. I can hardly sleep at
nights for worry and you say you will not forgive me. Is this
right in a Christian bishop? What are you for? I know you will
think again and say you do.

How can you say you do not believe in reincarnation when it is
in the Bible? Exodus chapter 20 verse 5 I the Lord your God
am a jealous God, visiting the iniquity of the fathers upon
the children to the third and the fourth generation. Do you
believe that God would punish you for something that your
grandfather had done? I do not. It means to your third and
fourth rebirth, of course. And did not people say that John
the Baptist and Jesus were both Elijah born again? Do you read
your Bible?

Think hard. You must see the signs that you were Guy Fawkes.
What do you do on November the Fifth every year? Do you go to
a bonfire? Are you anxious? Does the sight of that poor burned
man cause you to grieve? Or do you think it is a merry sight?
And my nephew Colin tells me you are a very High Church
Bishop. That is because you were once a Roman Catholic and
still feel the same feelings about your statues and such like.
And your poor knowledge of the Scriptures is the same. Roman
Catholics are not allowed to read the Bible. It is a forbidden
book for them. Guy Fawkes did not know his Scriptures.

You did not send the photgraph I asked you for. I will let you
have the cost if you will pop one in the post, please. I
specially want to see you before I come down to St Alban's at
the beginning of May. I don't want the shock of seeing you
again for the first time in this life without seeing a picture
of you first. Please send one. What date in the first week of
May would suit you best for a meeting?

I am very nervous that you will not find it in your heart to
forgive me. You do, don't you? Say you do. What star sign are
you?

Thank you. Till we meet again!

Francis Wagstaffe

The Bishop of St Albans
Abbey Gate House, St Albans, Hertfordshire AL3 4HD
ST ALBANS 53305

From the Bishop's Chaplain

8 April 1993

Dear Mr Wagstaffe

Thank you for your further letter to the Bishop.   I am afraid that he is
away at the moment and therefore unable to answer your letter himself but I
think there are one or two matters on which I can set your mind and
conscience straight a little.

First of all, I can assure you that the Bishop has no lack of forgiveness
in his heart for you. It is simply that it is difficult for him to offer
forgiveness when he does not feel that he has been offended against.   You
can be sure that he bears no ill will against you and will be horrified to
know that you have been losing sleep on his account.

Secondly, I think you have been misinformed about Bishop John.   He is not
a "very High Church bishop", but is an Evangelical who takes the study of
Scripture very seriously indeed.   In fact, he is an Old Testament scholar
and a Hebraist, which means that he has an intimate knowledge of the Old
Testament in its original language. And he would be able to assure you
that no interpreter of the Bible of any repute has ever suggested that
Exodus Chapter 20 points to a belief in reincarnation.   That passage comes
from a time when there was a sense of corporate and family guilt because of
sin.   The notion of a purely individual responsibility was one which came
later in Israel's self understanding, and you will see its development in
Ezekiel Chapter 18.   As to the New Testament, it may be that there were
some popular beliefs that John the Baptist and Jesus were one of the old
prophets "come again", but it was certainly not their own self
understanding (see e.g. John 1 v 21).

I have enclosed a photograph of the Bishop if it helps to set your mind at
rest.   I am afraid, though, that it is most unlikely that he will have
time for a personal meeting at the beginning of May as his diary is already
completely full. I am afraid that your question about the Bishop's star
sign shows that you are a prey to beliefs which are not orthodoxally
Christian and which, I am afraid, are most certainly not helping you come
to terms with reality.   This is a serious matter and one on which you
could well be helped by finding proper Christian counsel.   I am sure that
your local vicar or Christian minister would be only too pleased to help
you.

With all good wishes

Yours sincerely

Nick Moir

The Rev Nick Moir

Francis Wagstaffe Esq
28 Danesway
Beverley
East Riding

Francis Wagstaffe
28 Danesway
Beverley
East Riding
Yorkshire
HU17 7JQ

The Bishop of St Albans.
Abbey Gate House.
St Albans
Herts
AL3 4HD

14th April 1993

Dear Bishop,

I have just got your letter from your boy Nick. Will you say
thank you to him for me please.

He has tried to brush off my experiences, with the callowness
of youth, but you and I know better. I know now that you are
trying to deny the fears you feel. There is no need. Your
photograph is proof! I recognised you as soon as I saw it.

I have got my nephew, Colin, to make some copies of it, and he
has removed the bushes you are lurking in. Then I put in your
hat, beard and moustache. Look at it Bishop! Can there be any
doubt? That is the tormented face that looked out at me that
fateful day.

Do not deny it any longer. say you forgive me.

I have picked up the clue you made your boy Nick put in his
letter. He says you are a Herbalist with a special interest in
the remedies of the Old Testament. I am not a scholar, but my
hypnotherapist is also a herbalist. He was once an alchemist
in a previous life, and he says that those who still interest
themselves in natural remedies are in tune with their previous
lives and the ways they used to heal. He has looked at your
letter and says that you are not allowed to admit it because
you are a bishop, but that your interest in ancient herbalism
is a hint to me of your real feelings and your belief in
reincarnation. How long have you known about your previous
character? Were you a healer in the Old Testament? I have
looked up the reference to Ezekiel in my Bible, and it is
about the healing powers of sour grapes. Enough said! I can
take a hint.

Would you let me have a list of the times and dates and places
when you will be having confirmations during May, please. That
should stop your boy Nick from interfering in our plot.

Yours sincerely,

Francis Wagstaffe

Francis Wagstaffe
28 Danesway
Beverley
East Riding
Yorkshire
HU17 7JQ

The Bishop of Worcester,
Bishop's Palace,
Worcester.

3rd April 1993

Dear Bishop,

I intended to write to you last year, but Mrs Wagstaffe
prevented me. She said that no good would come of it. I read
in the newspaper that you had spoken to a conference of your
young people, and you had urged them to particiapate in
sexual experiments. As if that was not bad enough, you did so
in the most indelicate terms. 'Find it. Fuck it. Forget it.'
you said. I was incensed and should have written, but I paid
heed to my wife.

Now, I find that my niece Mavis has returned from a 'bargain
break' holiday in Weston-Super-Mare in a state of pregnancy.
She is unable to get in touch with the father of this child
because he gave her a false name and address. He followed your
advice!

Mavis is not a bad girl, and I doubt if she would ever have
got herself into such a scrape if the moral fibre of the
nation had not been eroded by the sort of teaching you and
your sort are giving. It makes me mad, I can tell you.

WHAT WORDS OF COMFORT DO YOU HAVE FOR HER NOW?

I believe I would be right to ask a solicitor if I can cite
you as an accessory before the fact and can claim a paternity
order against you in the absence of the father. After all,
conspirators to murder get the same penalty as the murderer.
Why should conspirators to immorality get different treatment
under the law? Answer me that! Did not Bentley hang for
shouting, 'let him have it'? You shouted such advice at your
youth conference, did you not?

I look forward to hearing what you indend to do for Mavis.

Yours sincerely,

Francis Wagstaffe

FROM THE BISHOP OF WORCESTER

TELEPHONE: HARTLEBURY (0299) 250214
FAX. NO: 0299 250027

THE BISHOP'S HOUSE
HARTLEBURY CASTLE,
KIDDERMINSTER,
WORCESTERSHIRE,
DY11 7XX

19th April 1993

Dear Mr. Wagstaffe,

The conference to which you refer in your letter of 3rd April was not one for young people and I certainly did not encourage those present to participate, as you put it, in sexual experiments.

I invited eighty people to my house to consider the future of marriage and the family. There were present at the gathering a cross-section of concerned people including social workers, teachers, magistrates, police, counsellors and clergy. The quotation described the anti-social, aggressive-towards-women behaviour which is unleashed on our society when marriage and the family break down.

In retrospect I realise it was foolish to use such a quotation, and particularly such an ugly word, since the press chose to sensationalise the event and this overshadowed what everyone agreed was an extremely useful and interesting day. The conference was unanimous that all concerned, including the media, have the duty to promote good marriage and stable family life.

Having said that, may I say how sorry I am to hear about your niece, Mavis and the situation in which she finds herself. I deplore the casual attitude to sex of many young people nowadays and can only repeat that I have never encouraged it.

Yours sincerely,

+Philip Worcester

Mr. Francis Wagstaffe,
28 Danesway,
Beverley,
East Riding,
Yorkshire, HU17 7JQ

Francis Wagstaffe
28 Danesway
Beverley
East Riding
Yorkshire
HU17 7JQ

The Bishop of Worcester,
The Bishop's House.
Hartlebury Castle
Kidderminster.
Worcestershire.
DY11 7XX

20th April 1993

Dear Bishop,

Thank you for your letter of 19th April. If what you say is
true about your meeting and the intention you had then you
have certainly set my mind at rest on that point. Though what
you think there is to be gained by meeting with rif-raff like
social workers, counsellors and teachers beats me! They seem
to behave worse than the children!

But, and here is the real point of my letter, I am very
distressed that you accuse my niece, Mavis, of having what you
call a 'casual attitude to sex'. I can assure you that she was
seduced by this young rascal. She is a good girl and has never
behaved like this before. It would break her heart if I told
her what you have said. In my letter to you I asked what words
of comfort you had for her. These, Sir, are not words of
comfort! May I plead with you again for a kind and early word?

I hope that with your advanced views on personal matters all
is well between you and your lady wife.

Yours sincerely,

Francis Wagstaffe

FROM THE BISHOP OF WORCESTER

TELEPHONE: HARTLEBURY (0299) 250214
FAX. NO: 0299 250027

THE BISHOP'S HOUSE
HARTLEBURY CASTLE.
KIDDERMINSTER,
WORCESTERSHIRE.
DY11 7XX

22nd April 1993

Dear Mr. Wagstaffe,

I am sorry if the final paragraph of my letter gave the impression that I was accusing your niece of casual sex. I was doing nothing of the kind. I was implying that it is difficult for young people in a world where casual attitudes towards sex exist, but I was not referring to her.

Please tell your niece, Mavis, how much I am concerned for her. I shall have her name on a card in my chapel so that I shall remember her each day in my prayers. I know that she will have the support of an affectionate family in the months and years that lie ahead. I also hope that she is a member of a lively church congregation which will give her the companionship and support she needs.

May God bless her.

Yours sincerely,

+ Philip Worcester

Mr. Francis Wagstaffe,
28 Danesway,
Beverley,
East Riding,
Yorkshire, HU17 7JQ

THE DIOCESE OF SOUTHWARK
THE BISHOP OF SOUTHWARK *The Rt Rev. Roy Williamson*

Bishop's House, 38 Tooting Bec Gardens,
Streatham, London SW16 1QZ
Tel: 081 769 3256 Fax: 081 769 4126

Friday 5th March 1993.

Dear Francis,

Thank you for your letter of the 22nd February which has just arrived with me via Coventry!

As you say I came "up through the ranks" and am very surprised to find myself as a Bishop in the Church of England. I had eighteen years in Nottingham before moving to be Bishop of Bradford. After nearly eight fairly exciting years in West Yorkshire I was 'translated' to Southwark nearly 15 months ago. Southwark is one of the largest dioceses in the C of E — with 2½ million people and nearly 600 clergy. Life is busy — and interesting.

I'm afraid that I haven't written any books about myself — it's not my style — but I have produced two little books in which I try to make the Christian faith intelligible to ordinary people. They are fairly single efforts but they have been well received and have sold well. I have enclosed a copy of each for you. They come with my compliments.

If you wanted to read just a little about my earlier life then you would need to look up Lord Longfords book called "The <u>Bishops</u>" published in 1986. in which he has a chapter on me.
A new paper back is just about to be published by Pan and written by Marica Porter, called "Dreams and Doorways". She has included a chapter about me.

One other thing that you might find interesting is a video called "Shepherd called Ray". It was part of the Central T.V. Encounter series and has been very well reviewed and received.

I hope you might find some of these things interesting and helppue. It was good to hear from a fellow Ulsterman. I have met up with a few others in the House of Lords.

All good wishes
Sincerly,
Roy Williamson

Francis Wagstaffe
28 Danesway
Beverley
East Riding
Yorkshire
HU17 7JQ

The Bishop of Southwark
38 Tooting Bec Gardens.
Streatham.
London.
SW16 1QZ

12th March 1993

Dear Bishop,

Thank you for your letter and for the two books. I call that
real kind of you.

I am sorry about all the mix up. I don't know how I can have
got in such a mess. I don't want to blame Colin, but you know
what young people are. The thing is, he said you couldn't be
the Bishop of Southwark. He said that the Bishop of Southwark
is one of those Old Etonians who didn't know his a..e from his
elbow, and that he had a terrible wife who gave him the run
around and thought she was the bishop. You can guess that I've
put him right on that one. Didn't he look stupid when I showed
him your books! Who do you think Colin got you mixed up with?
Are there two bishops of Southwark. I'm all a bit at sea.

I'm glad to hear that you're selling a lot of them. How much
money do you make? What do you do with it? Does it go to you
or does the Church make you give it to them because you write
them in the firm's time? It's all a bit iffy isn't it? I mean
you wouldn't even get them published if you weren't a bishop,
so I suppose the Church has got a point. Anyway, that's all
water under the bridge. I'm looking forward to reading them.

By the way. I'm not an Unlsterman. I don't know where you got
that idea. I can't stand them. Present company and Ian Paisley
excepted, of course.

Thank you again for the letter and the books.

Yours sincerely,

Francis Wagstaffe

Bishops House
Wed.

Dear Mr Wagstaffe,

In my husband's absence, I
am dealing with private mail +
thought I'd drop you a quick
note. We have been here for only
1½ years, so I expect your friend
was thinking of Roy's predecessor.
There is only one Bp of Southwark.
Southwark covers most of London
South River + stretches to Reigate +
London Diocese covers North River.
I hope that clears up the problem!
(Sorry you can't stand Ulstermen
that includes me too !)

Best wishes Anne Williamson

Francis Wagstaffe
28 Danesway
Beverley
East Riding
Yorkshire
HU17 7JQ

The Bishop of Southwark
38 Tooting Bec Gardens.
Streatham.
London.
SW16 1QZ

10th April 1993

Dear Bishop,

Will you thank your lady wife for me, please? It was good of
her to write to me and put me straight about who the man was
with the awful wife. What was his name?

I have been having a look through your books which you were
kind enough to send me. They're a bit deep and they are heavy
going, but I'm doing my best. I find the questions hard, but I
have not given up. Perhaps you will be good enough to let me
know how I am doing.

On page 42 you ask How would you explain to a child that Jesus
is not just like Paul Daniels only better?

I must say I got a bit confused with this one. Is it because
Paul Daniels is only a little man going thin on top, but Jesus
was big and had lots of hair? I can't say I like Paul Daniels
a lot, even if he is a Yorkshireman like me (sorry about the
thing about Ulstermen, I hope your wife didn't take it
personally). It just goes to show there's good and bad in
everyone, doesn't it? Now David Nixon was a good magician, and
he was tall. But he was bald as well, I suppose. Anyway, I
won't beat about the bush. Here is my answer. how many marks
do I get?

I would say to the child - 'Don't be stupid. Paul Daniels is a
little bald man with a wife young enough to be his daughter.
All right, he does good tricks, and he makes a lot of money.
we can't say who was better because there is no television of
Jesus to look at.'

Don't mind my feelings. Just let me know if I've got it right.

I think your books are wonderful though. Have you got a
picture of yourself you could sign and let me have? I don't
expect you are bald!

Your chum from Coventry let me down about some tickets for the
Buckingham Palace Garden Party. They are all the same same
these public scholboys. All talk.

Yours sincerely,

Francis Wagstaffe

Francis Wagstaffe

3 New Walk, Beverley, East Riding. Yorkshire.

Canon Michael Green,
Springboard Trust.
Church House.
Westminster.

26th March 1993

Dear Mr Green,

When my nephew Colin was up at the University he heard you
preach and said it was the most important day of his life! A
rather big claim I think for a young man who has been a
Venture Scout. Since then, he has been a devoted Christian and
was a corporal in the Jesus Army for a short while. He has
often tried to win me over to his way of thinking but without
success. Recently he challenged me to read your sermon and
still not believe! Well, Wagstaffe isn't a man to turn down a
challenge like that, so I said I'll have a go.

You needent worry. I will approach the sermon in a proper
frame of mind, and I will try to let it work its magic on me
as it did on Colin. Fairs fair.

It is the sermon about the way you were a dissolute young man
with a sofa. You will remember it. Colin says, the drift of it
is, that you had a sofa, and that you had so many sexual
conquests on it that you wore a dip in the middle of it. It
goes on to say that you Saw The Light and mended your ways. I
must say I admire your pluck for coming straight out with it
like that, but I suppose that sort of thing impresses young
minds. And what's wrong with a sowing a few wild oats anyway?
I raise my hat to you. I only wish Colin had taken that bit of
advice to heart the way he took to the pie-jaw. It might have
made him a bit more of a real man. By the way, he showed me a
photo of you once on the backof a paperback book. I see youre
bald, so that proves what they say!

Thanking you in anticipation.

Yours faithfully,

Francis Wagstaffe

Lambeth Palace   London SE1 7JU

Correspondence Address:
7 The Green
Chilwell,
Nottingham NG9 5BE

Tel: (0602) 431738
Fax: (0602) 431737

From: The Reverend
Dr. Michael Green

*Canon of Coventry Cathedral
and Adviser in Evangelism
to the Archbishops of
Canterbury and York*

13 April 1993

Dear Francis,

Thank you for your extremely entertaining letter. I am not sure that I can recall your nephew Colin, because we had five or six hundred students milling around our church most of the time. I am intrigued that he has a sermon still on tape from those days at university which must have been at least 10 years ago, because I have been in Canada since 1987.

I delight in your lively approach to life, and so I am sending you, with my best wishes, a direct hard–hitting little book which might interest you. But I am afraid I am ‚ going to have to disappoint you about the sofa with the dip in the middle. I had indeed an old sofa in my study but it had not worn old through masses of sexual conquests! It was infact a rather special place where scores of people knelt to entrust their lives to Christ! It is true that I had a fairly wild time before becoming a committed Christian: that included things like a little mild arson, but not fornication! So I am afraid we are going to have to find another reason for my baldness....

I really enjoyed hearing from you. Somebody with your guts and drive needs to be Christian. There are too many wimps around the Christian scene and there is a crying need for leadership in this bleeding country of ours. If you can't beat them (and you won't) why not join them?

Yours ever,

Michael Green.

`Springboard" is an initiative of the Archbishops of Canterbury and York for the Decade of Evangelism
Lambeth Fund. Charity No. 287211

Francis Wagstaffe

3 New Walk, Beverley, East Riding. Yorkshire.

Canon Michael Green,
7 The Green.
Chilwell
Nottingham.
NG9 5BE

14th April 193

Dear Mr Green,

I think I owe you an apology. What a fool you must think me. I
never said Colin had your sermon on tape. What I said was, I
wanted to read it, and I meant could you send me a copy. I
thought that was clear, but obviously not.

Thank you for the book. It loks very interesting. I have had a
look through and can't see the bit about your sofa. Have you
still got that sermon, because I'd love to see a copy. Colin
won't let me rest until I do.

I am sorry to hear that you are a convicted arsonist. But even
Saint Paul went to prison, so don't let that worry you. But I
have to beg to differ with you about the crime. For myself, I
think that arson is a very much more serious crime than what
you call fornication, and I call a bit of fun. Still, you've
served your time and paid your debt to society, so all that's
behind you now. What did you set fire to? Was anyone hurt?
It's a frightening thing fire.

You probably would remember Colin if you saw him again. He is
very distinctive! Unles your memory is as bad as your
arithmetic! You say you left England in 1987, so it must have
been at least ten years ago. come off it! That would make us
1997, by my sums.

I am glad to hear what you say about firm leadership, even if
I can't quite agree with a parson swearing, whatever you think
of the state of the country. It was a shame the Church did not
speak out clearly when we needed to hear it. Where was your
voice when we needed you to give a lead in bringing back
hanging for child molesters, murderers and communists. Where
was your voice when Mrs Thatcher was slung out? Every parson
in the country should have been in his pulpit urging people to
support her! It is a pity you confine your support to letters
and do not speak out! Give a lead! Christians support the
death penalty!

I've often thought I could write a book about my experiences
and philosophy of life, but I've been put off by the thought
of such a great undertaking. But now I've seen your book I
think I might be able to have a go. I didn't know they
published things of only 55 pages. Does it pay much? I'd be
grateful if you could give me the name of the chap at the
publishers when you send me the sermon.

Thanking you in anticipation.

Yours faithfully,

Francis Wagstaffe

Lambeth Palace London SE1 7JU

Correspondence Address:
7 The Green
Chilwell,
Nottingham NG9 5BE

Tel: (0602) 431738
Fax: (0602) 431737

From: The Reverend
Dr. Michael Green

*Canon of Coventry Cathedral
and Adviser in Evangelism
to the Archbishops of
Canterbury and York*

6 May 1993

Dear Mr. Wagstaff,

Thank you for your further letter. Michael Green is at present in New Zealand, hence I am replying on his behalf.

We don't actually have any copies of Michael Green's sermons at St. Aldate's. But if you could track down from Colin when it was that he heard this sermon, and then write to Canon David MacInnes, St. Aldate's Parish Centre, 40 Pembroke Street, Oxford OX1 1BP, someone would be able to let you know if it is still in the tape library. Sorry I can't be more help than that!

With best wishes,

Yours sincerely,

Jane Holloway

Jane Holloway
PA to Michael Green

Francis Wagstaffe

3 New Walk, Beverley, East Riding. Yorkshire

The Bishop of Lichfield,
Bishop's Palace,
Lichfield,
Staffordshire.

11th April 1993

Dear Bishop,

I am writing to you about a rather exciting discovery I have
made.

Recently, my aunt Evelyn died, leaving me her sole
beneficiary. She was not a wealthy woman, and I had lost all
hope of gaining anything worthwhile. Then while turning out a
cupboard, I found a cardboard box, sealed with brown tape.
Upon opening it, I discovered a receptacle with a glass front
and a sheaf of documents. Inside the receptacle was a
shriveled digit, like a human finger. On the back was a label,
in my aunt's hand, reading - Relic of St. Chad, once displayed
in the Cathedral Church of St Chad in Lichfield, where he was
the bisohop. Another label, not in her hand, read — membrum
Sancti Ceaddae virili. There was a document also in Latin,
which I am unable to read, but, affixed to it by a rusty paper
clip was another paper, again in my aunt's hand, which read —
document of certification of authenticity, signed by Pope Pius
the Twelfth. I assume he was a friend of St. Chad.

I am sure you, as Bishop of Lichfield, will be as excited by
this as I am. I am also sure that you share with me the desire
that it should be replaced in the cathedral where it belongs.
I must hasten to add that I am in do. doubt thatmy aunt was the
rightful owner of the piece, and that it is now in my lawful
posession.

I am not at all sure what the going rate is for the digit of a
saint, but I would like to give you first refusal as long as
you make a good offer. I am sure it will be worth your while.
Apart from the natural desire to have the thing restored to
its rightful place there is the question of increased takings
through added tourism to your Cathedral.

I can come to see you in Lichfield at the beginning of May, as
soon as I have cleared things up at this end. I will call in
and let you see the sacred object for yourself. Could you let
me know how much you are likely to offer, so that I can give
it some thought?

Francis Wagstaffe

From:

Captain David Brown OBE RN Rtd
The Bishop's Assistant

Telephone: 0543 262251

Facsimile: 0543 415801

Bishop's House
The Close
Lichfield
Staffordshire
WS13 7LG

16 April 1993

Mr Francis Wagstaffe
3 New Walk, Beverley
East Riding, Yorkshire

Dear Mr Wagstaffe,

I write to thank you on the Bishop's behalf for your recent letter.

I have passed it to the Cathedral Administrator, Mr James Wilson, who will get in touch with you once he has had a chance to look into the matters you raise.

Yours sincerely,

David Brown

Francis Wagstaffe

3 New Walk, Beverley, East Riding. Yorkshire

The Bishop of Lichfield,
Bishop's House
The Close,
Lichfield,
Staffordshire.
WS13 7LG

23rd April 1993

Dear Bishop,

I have got your letter from your Captain Brown, and I'm not
surprised to hear that you are very excited about my
discovery. It is none of business, I know, but don't you think
it looks a bit odd having a sailor as your assistant, living
at the same address! I know that the Church of England has
gone astray, but I thought that the example of the Bishop of
Gloucester would be a warning. Still, as I say, it's none of
my business. I only mention it because I wouldn't want any
suggestions of shady business interfering with our transaction
over Saint Chad.

I will be in Lichfield next weekend. I can call in on you,
with the sacred receptacle, either on the Saturday or the
Sunday. Saturday would be best, because it would give us time
to sleep on offers and negotiate. See you on the Saturday,
unless I hear that sunday is better.

Yours sincerely,

From:
Captain David Brown OBE RN Rtd
The Bishop's Assistant

Telephone: 0543 262251

Facsimile: 0543 415801

Bishop's House
The Close
Lichfield
Staffordshire
WS13 7LG

26 April 1993

Mr Francis Wagstaffe

Dear Mr Wagstaffe,

The Bishop has asked me to thank you for your
further letter of 23 April.

The Bishop regrets that he is unable to see you
during your visit to Lichfield.

Yours sincerely,

David Brown

Chapter Office, 14 The Close, Lichfield, Staffordshire WS13 7LD
Telephone: Lichfield 256120

From: Canon J. Howe

21 May 93

Dear Mr Wagstaffe,

The Bishop has handed on to the cathedral the correspondence concerning your discovery. Your find could indeed be very exciting and would be of interest to us. However I feel we need to know a little more about it.

Our records of relics displayed in the cathedral go back as far as 1345 and refer only to __bones__ of the saint, with no mention of a mummified relic of any kind. Moreover I doubt if this even claims to be a __finger__. I am no great classical scholar, but the Latin title means the "male member". If this is correct, we have an item most unlikely to have been displayed for the veneration of the faithful. Examination by experts is necessary to identify what the object is, and its date.

The documentary evidence on its own is weak. The certificate is modern (Pius XII died in 1958). Somehow you need to discover the evidence on which it was granted. Any details of how it came into your aunt's possession would help.

You mention market value. I have no idea of the secular market for curios. The Roman Catholic Church forbids the sale or purchase of sacred relics. The Churches of the Reformation objected to the mediaeval abuse of relics and even today have little interest in them unless there is a local connection with the saint.

My advice must be that there would be little ecclesiastical interest without further investigation of the item: what it is and its date, plus any evidence of a link with St Chad. I am sure you appreciate the necessity for such enquiry before we could properly be interested.

If you would like names of experts who could be consulted, I will gladly advise.

Thank you for thinking of us.

Yours sincerely

J.P. Hove

Francis Wagstaffe
28 Danesway
Beverley
East Riding
Yorkshire
HU17 7JQ

The Bishop of London.
Bishop's Palace.
London.

Dear Bishop,

I was delighted to see you on the popular television programme
'The Big Breakfast' last week. It is time that more of our
church leaders got down from their ivory towers and showed
they are prepared to speak to the common man, even if it was
only about how to keep mould off cheese. I was sorry that they
limited you to a small item, and kept you hanging around the
studio kicking your heels for only a few seconds of what I
believe is called 'air-time'. Still, it was better than
nothing and I bet you enjoyed seeing the media folk at work.

The point is though, that I think you may have a done a lot of
harm with your tip! I keep my cheese in a china dish on a
marble slab in the pantry. Putting it in the frig destroys its
taste and texture. So I have had a lot of trouble with mould.
I tried following your advice, and as soon as the programme
was over I slipped a couple of sugar lumps into the dish. To
my dismay, this morning when I looked in to see that it was
still free from mould, I found two maggots in the dish! This
has never happened before. I think it may be that the sugar
has attracted an early fly and tainted the cheese with its
eggs! Do you think you should go back on the programme and
explain to people that it is dangerous? I would think it would
be worth going back just to see that Gaby Roslin again. Who
knows, this time you might be able ot have an interview on the
bed with Paula Yates! Just the thing for a single man. Her
father was a bishop as well.

I am glad to have the opportunity to write to you, because I
have been interested to read that you are looking for the
names of Conservatives to promote to high office in the Church
of England. About time too! Here is my list.

Mr Geoffrey Dickens. M.P. He is a true conservative and cares
about family values and the English cup of tea. He is also
well-built and looks like an archdeacon.

Lord Archer. With his gift for language he could pep up the
services. He would be a good ambassador for the church abroad.
Make him a bishop.

Mr Nicholas Ridley M.P. He would sort out the moaning minnies
who think we should join with the methodists and such. No
Europe, no church unity! If they want to join us then let them
come on our terms! Nicholas Ridley could run Westminster
Abbey. That would put a stop to pagan worship in our premier
royal chapel!

Lord Tebbitt. The Archbishop of Canterbury clearly is not up
to the job. Lord Tebbitt could pull the thing into shape. He
would put the church commissioners on their toes and make them
make a profit. All right, he got some stick when he was
Chairman on the Party, but HE WON US THE ELECTION!

Lord David Owen. This is not as surprising as you might think.
He is a healer, a diplomat, a uniter. Send him to Northern
Ireland to blow the paddies out of the water! He would soon
have peace in that troubled land. He could be Archbishop of
Dublin. His wife is an American and she could help him to have
a word with President so-called Bill Clinton and tell him to
keep his nose out.

I would on no account appoint Mr John so-called Selwyn Gummer
to any post. Any man who feeds his daughter mad cow disease is
not to be trusted. And his eyes are too close together.

Yours sincerely,

copies to:

Geoffrey Dickens MP
Lord Archer
Nicholas Ridley MP
Lord Tebbitt
Lord David Owen
John Gummer MP

FROM
THE BISHOP OF LONDON

LONDON HOUSE
8 BARTON STREET
WESTMINSTER SW1P 3NE
TELEPHONE : 071-222 8661
FAX : 071-799 2629

Francis Wagstaffe
28 Danesway
BEVERLEY
Yorkshire
HU17 7JQ

28 April 1993

Dear Francis Wagstaffe,

Thank you for your letter and comments. I am sorry to hear of your experience following my tip on The Big Breakfast about the two sugar lumps in the cheese dish. I don't actually think there is any chance of a further interview. It does take quite a bit of time even to achieve a minute's viewing on the television!

In fact it was something I remember my mother doing but that was well before the days of fridges, when it was always kept in the kitchen pantry downstairs. I don't recall any problems with flies or maggots, but then I do not claim to be any expert in these matters.

With greetings and all good wishes,

Yours sincerely,

Francis Wagstaffe

28 Danesway, Beverley, East Riding, Yorkshire.

The Bishop of Newcastle,
Bishop's House,
Moor Road South,
Newcastle.
NE3 !PA

29th April 1993

Dear Bishop,

My nephew, Colin, who worked as a waiter in the Carlton Club
(<u>London SW1</u> not one of your sleasy clip joints but a place
where decent grammar school boys go to have dinner), says he
overheard one of the members say that you were a first rate
Tory. I'm glad to hear it. I was the proprietor of a prep
school for many years (Potter Hall, famous in the East Riding)
and then I sank the proceeds in a pork butcher's, so I know
how small businesses need firm government. I can now rank you
with the Bishop of Peterborough and Stanley Booth-Whatsit as
the only sound prelates on the bench. Of course Dr Westwood
has my further admiration (given that he is as short as you
are) in offering his services in the South Atlantic in 1982
"to stick one up the Argies". Isn't it amazing to think that
someone of his age was prepared to make a sea journey of any
sort, let alone a trip of 6,000 miles?

The reason that I am writing to you rather than Dr Westwood is
that since he is broadcasting regularly and is frequently in
the House of Lords he is a very busy man, and you, I know, as
a bachelor in the sticks will have the time to deal with my
enquiry.

Until silly ruomours, of the sort that circulate in the
Movement these days, I was a Group Scout Leader in the East
Riding. I sometimes despair of the organization founded by
Baden-Powell - he was a good Tory too of course and knew how
to put the "you know whats" in their place. (He'd have been
out there with Dr Westwood). I think it is now time to have a
new all-boys organization liberated from the restrictive old-
fashioned sexual morality which causes such unnecessary
gossip. We need an organization which will attract healthy,
well-bodied lads, using the principles inspired by Powell,
discipline and self-control, the curbing of beastliness.

Colin's friend, Kevin, who is big in leather in Northampton,
has offered to cost out the uniform I have designed. I am
happy to let you have pen drawings.

I think you would be the ideal man to lead my new organization
and give it the national impetus it would require. Would you
agree to be the man I have decided to call 'The Fair Leader'?
My Neice, Mavis, lives in Craster, where the crabs come from,
and I've got to go up there for a Masonic do in Ashington on
the 16th, so I'll be virtually passing your door. I shall drop
in on the way up, or on the way back, depending on the
traffic, to discuss further details.

Yours sincerley,

Francis Wagstaffe

PS. Wait till you see the Fair Leader's uniform!

From the
Bishop of Newcastle

Bishop's House
29 Moor Road South
Newcastle upon Tyne
NE3 1PA

Telephone:
(091) 285 2220

4th May, 1993

F. Wagstaffe, Esq.
28 Danesway
Beverley
East Riding

Dear Mr Wagstaffe,

   I am writing to thank you for your letter of 29th April which
I must confess caused me some surprise.   You are certainly right
about my political views, but I very much doubt if I am the right
person for your new organization.   I do not have much to do with
youth organizations, and I think that you really need to look for
someone who has a younger and more popular image.   I note that
you will be coming up to Northumberland on the 16th, but as that
is a Sunday I shall be out and about the diocese on that day and
I therefore very much doubt whether our paths will cross.

   With every good wish,

                    Yours sincerely,

Francis Wagstaffe

28 Danesway, Beverley, East Riding, Yorkshire.

The Bishop of Newcastle,
Bishop's House,
Moor Road South,
Newcastle.
NE3 1PA

17th May 1993

Dear Bishop,

Thnak you for your letter. I am sorry that you don't feel able
to offer yourself as our Fair Leader, but I take your point!

I had a lovely weekend at Craster (and looked longingly at
your door as I passed).

I have talked to my nephew, Colin, about what you said about a
younger image, and we have come up with three ideas.

Cliff Richard (who is a good example to the young and who I
like very much.)

Julian Clary (who I have never heard of, but who Colin's
friend Kevin says would be ideal and would look good in the
uniform).

Which one do you think? Or would they both be equally
suitable? I am sorry to bother you again, but you have been so
kind.

By the way, as a Tory and a leader, what do you think Mr Major
should do with the Cabinet? Is it time to ditch Lamont? I
don't think I could vote for them at the moment and I would
value your views.

Yours sincerely,

Francis Wagstaffe

From the
Bishop of Newcastle

Bishop's House
29 Moor Road South
Newcastle upon Tyne
NE3 1PA

Telephone:
(091) 285 2220

20th May, 1993

Francis Wagstaffe, Esq.
28 Danesway
Beverley,   East Riding

Dear Mr Wagstaffe,

Thank you very much for your letter of 17th May.   It is good to
hear that you had an enjoyable weekend in Northumberland recently.   On
the Sunday afternoon I was on the banks of the Tweed and saw the Cheviot
range covered in snow.

Alas, I cannot help you with advice about the names whom you mention
in your letter, for I really do not know sufficient about them.

With every good wish,
                    Yours sincerely,

Francis Wagstaffe
28 Danesway
Beverley
East Riding
Yorkshire
HU17 7JQ

The Bishop of Norwich,
Bishop's Palace.
Norwich.
Norfolk.

10th April 1993

Dear Bishop,

I hope you do not mind me writing to you, but I have a
proposal which I think you will find it impossible to refuse.
I am sure you watch the splendid American television programme
BAYWATCH every Saturday night. If you do not, then let me
commend it to you. It is set in California and it features
attractive specimens of young men and women, in bathing
costumes. The idea of the programme is that they are
lifeguards and each episode is an exciting adventure in the
life of a lifeguard. The adventures are rather flimsy and the
real point of the programme is the tanned young bodies in
swimming costumes. It is very popular.

I have some experience as a writer. I was a Group Scout Leader
for several years until I felt that I ought to retire from
that post. Scouting is not what it was, I regret to say, and
there are many petty jealousies which can lead to unpleasant
rumours! In my capacity as Group Scout Leader I edited the
newsletter, and I wrote many an uplifting story of Venture
Scouts, their young bodies and their exploits. I think that an
English programme, based on the BAYWATCH formula would be a
great commercial success, and we could give it a more moral
slant than the American version.

My nephew Colin has some experience of leading beach missions
in Wales. Put the two together and what have you got? The new,
exciting programme BEACH MISSION! The young evangelists could
patrol the beach in their skimpy costumes, attracting young
viewers, then when they had got their interest, they could
slam home the gospel message. There is many an exciting
possibility on every beach.

I think that the new television companies would leap at this
opportunity to make money and promote themselves as caring,
sharing people. The ideal situation for this dynamic new show
would be Great Yarmouth. I am sure that with your name on the
package we could get the companies bidding against each other
in a competitive auction. Will you come in with us?
I have to warn you that I am sending a copy of this letter to
my nephew, Colin, so that the copyright is protected! I know
how easy it is to filch ideas in the media world.

I enclose a copy of the first page of my proposals.

Yours sincerely,

Francis Wagstaffe

FRANCIS WAGSTAFFE

AND

THE BISHOP OF NORWICH

PRESENT

BEACH MISSION

an exciting new drama series
about
the thrills and spills
of a team
of teenage evanglelists

WRITER/PRODUCER

Francis Wagstaffe

DIRECTOR

Colin Wagstaffe

THEOLOGICAL CONSULTANT

The Bishop of Norwich

BISHOP'S HOUSE

NORWICH

NR3 1SB

(0603) 614172

The Revd Michael Stagg

Bishop's Chaplain and
Diocesan Communications Officer

19th April, 1993

Francis Wagstaffe, Esq.,
28 Danesway
Beverley
East Riding
Yorkshire
HU17 7JQ

Dear Mr. Wagstaffe,

Bishop Peter has asked me to thank you for your letter of the 10th
April. He was interested in your proposals for a new television
programme but it is not his practice to lend his support to such
schemes.

Yours sincerely,

Francis Wagstaffe
28 Danesway
Beverley
East Riding
Yorkshire
HU17 7JQ

The Bishop of Norwich,
Bishop's Palace.
Norwich.
Norfolk.
NR3 1SB

23rd April 1993

Dear Bishop,

I have the letter form your communications officer, and I am
delighted that although you do not usually lend your name to
such projects as BEACH MISSION you are interested in my
proposal, so you want to go ahead. I think it's wise and far-
sighted of you. I'll get the Press Releases out straight away.

I've also been thinking a little about casting. We were hpoing
to have the late Cardew Robinson for the part of the Bishop
who commissions the young evangelists in the pilot programme,
but sadly his recent death has robbed us of his talents. So,
it would be a good attention catcher for the series if you
would take this role. It is a cameo role, and won't involve
more than the usual acting skills any Bishop uses - you'll
just need to pin on the badges on to their swimming costumes,
wear a fixed smile and keep your hand on your ha'penny.

We are targetting all the major new production companies, and
I expect to have some positive responses for you very soon.

Yours sincerely,

Francis Wagstaffe

FRANCIS WAGSTAFFE

AND

THE BISHOP OF NORWICH

PRESENT

BEACH MISSION

an exciting new drama series
about
the thrills and spills
of a team
of teenage evanglelists

WRITER/PRODUCER

Francis Wagstaffe

DIRECTOR

Colin Wagstaffe

THEOLOGICAL CONSULTANT

The Bishop of Norwich

AND

introducing

THE BISHOP OF NORWICH

in

the role of

THE COMISSIONER

BISHOP'S HOUSE
NORWICH
NR3 1SB
(0603) 614172

The Revd Michael Stagg

Bishop's Chaplain and
Diocesan Communications Officer

26th April 1993

Mr Francis Wagstaffe,
28 Danesway,
Beverley,
East Riding,
Yorks. HU17 7JQ

Dear Mr Wagstaffe,

Thank you for your letter 23rd April to Bishop Peter. I am sorry you
have clearly misunderstood what I wrote to you. Your project is **not** one
he can endorse. It is important that you do not use his name in **any**
publicity material. My letter did not give you such permission so
please do not do so.

Yours sincerely

Francis Wagstaffe
28 Danesway
Beverley
East Riding
Yorkshire
HU17 7JQ

The Bishop of Norwich,
Bishop's Palace.
Norwich.
Norfolk.
NR3 1SB

26th April 1993

Dear Bishop,

I am bit flumoxed by a letter I have just received from your
communications officer. He says that you did not give your
approval to our project, but in his first letter he said 'He
was interested in your proposals for a new television
programme.' Now you can't get clearer than that, can you? Why
has he changed his mind?

The problem is, I have already sent out the proposal to the TV
companies on the strength of your first approval. It would
look odd of you to try to change your mind now, wouldn't it?
Is it the Cardew Robinson role that's worrying you? You will
be excellent in it and it will show how the Church is involved
in,real issues. BEACH MISSION will be a success. Leave the
arrangements to me.

Yours sincerely,

Francis Wagstaffe

Francis Wagstaffe
28 Danesway
Beverley
East Riding
Yorkshire
HU17 7JQ

The Bishop of Norwich,
Bishop's Palace.
Norwich.
Norfolk.
NR3 1SB

17th May 1993

Dear Bishop,

I thought I would keep you up to date on the progress of our
project. I have heard today from Euston Films, who are very
interested in the particular genre we are working in, but are
fully committed with their own programmes in this field at the
moment.

That's tha bad news. But the good news is that he has put me
on to London Weekend Television, so I'll let you know how we
get on there. (It's also with about half a dozen other people
who are still considering it, costing it out, and checking
casting, storylines, etc.). I'll keep you posted.

I'm glad you've lost your cold feet on it!

Yours sincerely,

Francis Wagstaffe

Francis Wagstaffe

3 New Walk, Beverley, East Riding, Yorkshire.

The Head of Drama,
Euston Films Ltd.,
365 Euston Road,
NW1 3AR.

24th April 1993

Dear Sir,

I am happy to be able to offer you the opportunity of putting in a bid for
our exciting new drama series BEACH MISSION.

As you will see, we have put together a package which offers the viewing
public the cocktail of ingredients which most interest today's young
people - a seaside setting, attractive young bodies in swimming costumes,
and the search for meaning in life. A search I have recently undertaken
myself. We are lucky to have been able to secure the services of the
Bishop of Norwich as our Theological Consultant and as the shadowy figure
of 'The Comissioner' (the sort of Charlie figure from CHARLIE'S ANGELS).

I feel sure you will see what a winner this idea will be. I have myself
considerable experience in judging the mood of the public and making money
out its needs and desires. For many years I ran a successful Prep School
(Potter Hall - famous in the East Riding), and then made my money grow in
the pork butcher's trade. Recently, I have put aside fleshly interests
(like prepschoolmastering) and have become interested in the things of the
spirit. I have been able to buy outright a local church (The Old Northern
Catholick Church of the East Riding, and I am expecting many to flock to
us when the Church of England ordains priestesses. We are on a promise
from the Archbishop of Canterbury. I also have an elevated title in the
Church which I do not use in business correspondence). This spiritual
quest has led me down many in interesting alley and will provide an
endless source of strong story lines for the series BEACH MISSION. We
will take the young viewers through the quest, with issues such as
reincarnation, personal relationships beyond the pale, race meetings
dyslexia and uniformed youth organisations. It's a winner and a sure
moneymaker. I advise you to get in on the ground floor.

If the right bid came in I am pretty sure we could also enlist the
services of the famous bald evangelist and mild arsonist Canon Michael
Green, who has a large network of contacts among our target audience of
youngster!

I look forward to hearing from you.

Yours faithfully,

Francis Wagstaffe

13 May 1993

Mr. Francis Wagstaffe
3 New Walk
Beverley
East Riding
Yorkshire

Dear Mr Wagstaffe,

Thank you very much for your letter dated 24 April,
which arrived only on 10 May, and for giving us the
opportunity to invest in BEACH MISSION.

Unfortunately here at Euston Films we have already
embarked on several projects which combine fervent
evangelism with ratings-buster storylines and marquee
casting. For example, the BBC has expressed strong
interest in our twice-weekly serial CROOKSIDE, which
probes the lives, loves, heartaches and conscience
crises of six ecclesiastical families who live as
neighbours in a cathedral close. ITV are equally keen
on our new 9.00 pm drama series PRIEST SQUAD, starring
John Thaw as the leader of a no-holds-barred team of
troubleshooting vicars. So you can see that
regrettably we have no room for further ventures in
this exciting genre.

However I imagine your idea would go down tremendously
well at London Weekend Television, where the recent
creation of several millionaires among the executives
must lead inevitably to a re-examination of moral and
religious values in the programme output. You should
address your letter to Mr Melvyn Bragg, who will
surely be the first to feel the call of the spirit.

Yours sincerely,

JOHN HAMBLEY

EUSTON FILMS LIMITED 365 Euston Road
London
NW1 3AR

Telephone 071-387 0911
Facsimile 071-388 2122

Registered Address 306-316 Euston Road
London NW1 3BB
Registration Number 1005255 Registered in England
A THAMES TELEVISION COMPANY

Francis Wagstaffe
28 Danesway
Beverley
East Riding
Yorkshire
HU17 7JQ

Melvyn Bragg
London Weekend Television
South Bank Television Centre
Kent House
Upper Ground.
London.
SE1 9LT

17th May 1993

Dear Mr Bragg,

I am writing to you at the suggestion of Mr John Hambley of
Euston films, who suggests you would be interested in our new
series BEACH MISSION. I enclose the proposals. I think you'll
agree it's a real money-spinner!

Strictly entre-nous, Mr Hambley is casting John Thaw as a no-
holds-barred vicar. I would have thought that after the last
turkey he would have stayed well clear of Thaw. So, we're one
up on him from the start. The Bishop of Norwich will be the
new Cardew Robinson of the nineties. Don't miss your chance.

The series will be shot in Great Yarmouth, and I can promise
you that the town council will give you every support and
encouragement. These resorts are on hard times, and the
opportunity to become 'Wagstaffe Country' will tempt them to
cast their bread upon the waters.

My nephew, Colin, who has heard of you before, says you come
from the north and used to do a chat show under the name of
Russell Harty, so you'll know that ordinary people are
interested in things of the spirit combined with local
interest and young evangelists in bathing costumes. I recently
completed my own Spiritual Quest and became the leader of a
local church, but that's another tale, but believe you me, I
know the market for religion!

Yours sincerely,

P. S. What is marquee casting?

Francis Wagstaffe
28 Danesway
Beverley
East Riding
Yorkshire
HU17 7JQ

The Bishop of Hereford,
Bishop's Palace.
Hereford.

10th May 1993

Dear Bishop, or perhaps I should say - Hi, Biker!

Like you, My nephew Colin and I are keen motor cycle
enthusiasts - I ride a BSA. I recently acquired sole ownership
of a local church (The Old Northern Catholick Church of the
East Riding) and am waiting for the influx of new members when
the C of E ordains priestesses. I want to set up a hardship
fund for parsons coming over with no private means, and have
been looking for a way of raising money. Colin's friend,
Kevin, who works on a cider farm near Ledbury, suggested a
brilliant idea. What we plan is to come down on our bike, with
the side-car, and get sponsorship to take you to all the pubs
in the diocese named THE MITRE!, (sitting in the side-car
wearing yours), and see how many we can fit in in three hours.
(I thought we ought not to take any longer because your diary
must be fairly full).

Please let me make it quite clear that there is no need for
you to have a drink in every one as Colin and I are going to
do. Apart from anything else, it would be bad for your image.
Instead, you can sit in the car park, waving and smiling to
the customers and rattling your collecting tin. I know you
will be pleased to help to provide for parsons who are hard up
because of the vote.

I think it is a genius of a scheme. We are going down to see
Kevin on the 18th May, so we'll be virtually passing your
door. We'll look in about lunch time and discuss the plan with
you.

Yours sincerely,

Francis Wagstaffe

P.S. Please do not offer Colin anything alcoholic to drink.
Once they get together on the farm there is no knowing what he
and Kevin will get up to with a few drinks in them!

Francis Wagstaffe
28 Danesway
Beverley
East Riding
Yorkshire
HU17 7JQ

The Bishop of Hereford,
Bishop's Palace.
Hereford.

9th June 1993

Dear Bishop,

Sorry I didn't manage to get in to see you on the 18th. Colin
and his friend Kevin exchanged harsh words and we had to spend
a little more time than we had planned trying to get them to
see sense. Still, that's all water under the bridge now and
they are on terms again, thank goodness. Young people!

Kevin has said he can pop round some of your local pubs with
the enclosed posters, getting a bit of interest up in your
visit. I've sent him fifty. I think they're pretty good,
don't you?

We're aiming at a date in the first fortnight in July. When
would suit you best?

With best wishes and Yorkshire blessings,

Yours sincerely,

Francis Wagstaffe

The Most Reverend Francis Wagstaffe
Archbishop of the Old Northern Catholick Church
of the East Riding
Metropolitan and Primate
Order of St. John of Beverley (First class)

BISHOP OF HEREFORD THE GEORD

will be visiting
your local,
collecting money for

THE OLD NORTHERN
CATHOLICK CHURCH
OF THE EAST RIDING

Please give generously

Francis Wagstaffe

3 New Walk
Beverley
East Riding
Yorkshire.

The Archbishop of Canterbury
Lambeth Palace
LONDON

29th January 1993 - St Gildas the Wise

Your Grace,

As a fellow Archbishop, may I offer you the hand of friendship and the
Greeting of Peace. You have been much in my thoughts and prayers in recent
months and it has been with great sadness that I have watched your Church
sink into apostasy and heresy over the priestess issue.

I think I may have an idea which will help you in the future. You may not
have heard of the Old Northern Catholick Church of the East Riding, but I
can assure you that we have fully valid, if irregular, orders which date
back to the Malines controversy and were bestowed on our Founder by Mar
Gregorius in Driffield. I am now the Metropolitan, and I have all the
documents and certificates which would be necessary to prove authenticity.
I am sure you will appreciate that I can not send them to you through the
post but I will gladly bring them with me when I come to see you. I myself
became an Old Northern Catholick when 'Honest to God' was published.
Dishonest to God, I call it.

We follow the traditional rite, based on the Prayer Book of 1549, with full
Catholick privileges, but we are not in any way obscurantist or inflexible
and would be willing to enter into discussion about adopting alternative
rites (but NOT the ASB!) in preparation for the first priests who would be
coming to us.

What I am proposing, is that I become the visiting Ordinary in the Northern
Province. We do not have representation south of Lichfield because of our
traditional adherence to the North, but I think it would be only fair of me
to offer to consecrate one of your senior men in the Southern Province and
give him full Vicar-General status. With your support I think we could use
Beverley Minster as our Pro-Cathedral. I can assure you that the people of
the East Riding would love to see a restoration of its status and would
flock to us.

I think that this will be the solution to your problems. Your people will
not need to look abroad for a home, but can be cared for here in ENGLAND,
where we belong. We can safeguard the future of the ENGLISH CHURCH. Time
is running short, and it may soon be TOO LATE! We have never had any
policy of reception of Anglicans when they join our Church, recognising as
we do the full Catholicity of Anglican orders and sacraments, so no one
will need to make any recantation or submission. Of course, this position
will change at the very second when the first woman is made a priestess in

your Church, so those who wish to avail themselves of our jurisdiction
must act soon. I have a shrewd suspicion that you were surprised when the
vote went through. I believe you are more intelligent that the press makes
out and that you are not too happy about the turn things have taken.

I have prepared a Press Release explaining this proposal, and will be
sending it out as soon as I have heard from you that you are interested in
talks. Of course, you will understand that I can not show you the full
text of this, as that would smack of collusion, and we could not allow
that. Please could you let me know when you like us to meet to discuss
arrangements, and I'll time the announcement to fit in with that. If I
don't hear from you I'll assume that that means you want to go ahead but
can't commit yourself straight away, but I'll give the press an indication
that you're favourable. I am retired now and so my diary is probably more
clear than yours.

Yours in Christ,

+ Francis Wagstaffe.

The Most Reverend Francis Wagstaffe - Metropolitan and Primate, Old
Catholick Church of the East Riding. Order of St. John of Beverley.

Bishop at Lambeth
The Right Reverend John Yates

Lambeth Palace
London SE1 7JU
tel: 071-928 8282
fax: 071-261 9836

11th February 1993

Your Grace,

The Archbishop of Canterbury has asked me to reply to your letter. The
recent proposals of the House of Bishops which included the suggestion
of Provincial Visitors are at present under discussion more widely
within the Church. I am instructed to say that it is thought unlikely
that recourse will be had to churches such as your own in this
connection, but of course your suggestion will be borne in mind.

I am sorry that the Archbishop's diary is too full for the foreseeable
future to take up your kind suggestion of a meeting. The matter would
in any case, of course, be of more direct concern to the Province of
York than to the Province of Canterbury.

Yours sincerely,

+ John~ce

The Most Revd Francis Wagstaffe
3 New Walk
Beverley
East Riding
Yorkshire

Francis Wagstaffe

3 New Walk
Beverley
East Riding
Yorkshire.

The Right Reverend John Yates
The Bishop at Lambeth
Lambeth Palace
LONDON
SE1 7JU

21st February 1993 - SS. Maurice, Photinus, Theodore and
Companions, MM.

Dear Bishop Yates,

Thank you for your letter of 11th February. I apologise for
the delay in replying, but I only received it on my return to
Yorkshire after a short spell in Derbyshire at our Oratory,
where I received a whole family into the Old Northern
Catholick Church of the East Riding, and at the same time
appointed an Archimandrite for the Kingdom of Mercia. The
Lord adds daily to our numbers.

I was a little surprised that the Archbishop did not reply
himself to my letter, but I have discussed it with my
colleagues and the general opinion seems to be that he
welcomes my suggestion, but that as matters are delicate at
the moment he prefers not to be too involved personally, in
case people think he is taking sides. I think this is a sound
move.

Reading between the lines, I take 'your suggestion will be
borne in mind' to mean that he is going to instruct the other
bishops to accept my plan, but he has to go through the
motions of referring it to them. I sometimes do the same
thing myself. I also interpret 'The matter would.....be of
more direct concern to the Province of York' to mean that he
is going to give me jurisdiction up here but that he has
someone else in mind for down south. I don't mind that at
all. After all, it makes sense not to put all your eggs in
one basket.

Following on from your letter, I'm now able to let you have a
look at the Press Release. I can see why you're acting up
front in this, it makes it look as though there's no collusion
between the East Riding and Canterbury. It makes it easier
for us to do a deal. I'll be sending it out on March 1st,
because that would be the feast of St. Oswald of York, if this
was a leap year (Feb 29th). That seems to me to be very
appropriate, even providential, don't you think? ('His purple
and gold stole was preserved in Beverley Minster, in the time
of Thomas Stubbs, who mentions the fact in his account of the
Archbishops of York') Lost now, I imagine!

You will always be a welcome guest in the East Riding, or
even, dare I suggest, a member of our heirarchy!

Yours sincerely,

Francis Wagstaffe

The Most Reverend Francis Wagstaffe - Metropolitan and
Primate, Old Catholick Church of the East Riding. Order of
St. John of Beverley.

Francis Wagstaffe

PRESS RELEASE

OLD NORTHERN CATHOLICK CHURCH OF THE EAST RIDING
TO CARE FOR PRIESTS DRIVEN OUT
OF THE CHURCH OF ENGLAND
BY THE PRIESTESS HERESY

THe Old Northern Catholick Church of the East Riding has
entered into discussions with Lambeth Palace about providing
alternative episcopal oversight for traditionalist priests.

The priests will not have to renounce former vows or take new
orders, but will be recognised by the Hierarchy and People of
the ONCCER.

A Spokesman for the Archbishop of Canterbury has said that the
proposals from Old Northern Catholicks 'will be borne in
mind' when the Provincial Visitors are discussed 'widely
within the Church'.

The scheme will not operate, at the spokesman's suggestion, in
the Southern Province, where other arrangements are in hand,
but is 'of direct concern to the Province of York'.

The Old Northern Catholick Church will provide a safe haven
for English Christians betrayed by the Synod, and will prevent
the need for traditionalists to submit themselves to the yoke
of Rome.

For more information, please contact:

The Most Reverend Francis Wagstaffe - Metropolitan and
Primate, Old Catholic Church of the East Riding. Order of
St. John of Beverley.

or:

The Right Reverend John Yates.
Lambeth Palace

Francis Wagstaffe

3 New Walk
Beverley
East Riding
Yorkshire.

The Archbishop of Canterbury,
Lambeth Palace
LONDON
SE1 7JU

1st March 1993

Dear Dr. Carey,

I am writing to you on behalf of my brother, Francis
Wagstaffe, and on his instructions.

Francis has been taken into hospital for surgery. We are
surprised that his appointment has come so soon, but he has
been many months on the waiting list and must not miss the
opportunity now that it has arisen.

He is very distressed that this has interfered with his work
with you and has asked me to let you know that he will resume
the discussions as soon as he is recovered. This should only
be a matter of a few weeks. I am preparing our House in
Derbyshire for his convalescence.

May I add a few words of my own, before I close this letter?
Do you think it wise, or kind, to ask him to bear so heavy a
burden at his time of life? Apart from this small matter of
his operation, he is in good health for his time of life, but
I do fear that he should not be asked to take such great
responsibilities as you have asked of him. He is willing to
serve, and will not let you down, as long as he is spared.

I have for many years acted as his secretary, so I know what
is being planned, although I am not myself a member of his
Church or yours. My mother taught us that there is only one
mediator between God and Man — JESUS CHRIST, and I need no
priests or archbishops, whether they be in Beverley or
Canterbury, my own family or strangers! I apologise for
speaking to you so plainly, but I am worried about what you
will do to my brother with your demands on him.

He does not know that I am adding this personal note to his
message, and I know you will respect it. I think you should
also know that he was disappointed that you should have asked
your assistant to reply to his letter to you. He understood
the political reason behind it, as he has said in his reply,
but he still felt hurt that no personal greeting should have
come to him in your own name and in your own hand. I know he
holds you in very high regard. He feels he can trust you
where he could not have confidence in your Bishop Yates. He

is not at all sure that Bishop Yates has passed on the Press
Release to you, and Francis is unsure whether to send it out
before you have approved it. I have advised him that he
should, but still he hesitates, lest he say something wrong.
What wording would you advise? Although I do not belong to
your church I weep to see what is happening to it as it slips
into decay and apostasy, so I am VERY ANXIOUS that Francis
should help in some way if no one else will save it.

Please accept my apologies for this rambling letter. I do not
have the concentration or clarity of thought which my brother
possesses. Do you agree with him, that women are the weaker
vessels? I certainly do. Saint Paul makes it clear in Holy
Scripture that we must serve. Would you take instruction from
a woman? I am sure you would not! Do you think the noble
Thomas Cranmer would have approved of the ordination of women?
I do not!

Before I finish, may I thank you for your patience, and make
one more request? It would mean so much to Francis if you
could let him have a signed photograph of yourself. We would,
of course, reimburse you for any expense this might cause you.

Yours sincerely,

Evelyn Wagstaffe

Evelyn Wagstaffe   (Miss)

Bishop at Lambeth
The Right Reverend John Yates

Lambeth Palace
London SE1 7JU
tel: 071-928 8282
fax: 071-261 9836

8 March 1993

Dear Miss Wagstaffe

I have to write again on behalf of the Archbishop of Canterbury. I am sorry to hear that your brother has had to be hospitalised and hope that he will recover quickly and completely. At the same time, I'm afraid both you and he have to accept that the Archbishop's heavy list of engagements and other correspondence makes it inevitable that he should delegate certain tasks to members of his staff.

I enclose a letter which was dictated before I received your letter and in reply to your brother's letter of 21 February. As background, it may help to summarise our correspondence. We received a letter dated 29 January. It contained a proposal from your brother that he should become what he described as the 'visiting Ordinary in the Northern Province'. In my reply dated 11 February I said that 'it is thought unlikely that recourse will be had to Churches such as your own in this connection ...'. His letter dated 21 February was therefore a surprise. Perhaps your brother was already unwell at that time and had misunderstood of misinterpreted my letter.

Quite simply, the Church of England has no plans to liaise in this way with Old Catholic Churches in the particular field of the Church's ministry to those opposed to the ordination of women, committed as we are to the ecumenical quest in general. It is consequently something of a surprise to read that you are suggesting that the Church of England is making untoward demands upon your brother. I am sure that his convalescence should not be threatened by having to add a continuation of this correspondence to the duties in connection with his own Church which will no doubt await him on his return from hospital.

With good wishes.

Yours sincerely

+ John Yates

Miss Evelyn Wagstaffe
3 New Walk
Beverley
EAST RIDING
Yorkshire

113

Bishop at Lambeth
The Right Reverend John Yates

Lambeth Palace
London SE1 7JU
tel: 071-928 8282
fax: 071-261 9836

8 March 1993

Dear Archbishop

Thank you for your letter dated 21 February. I understand the interpretation which you have placed upon my previous letter, but have to say plainly that the Archbishop would not be able in any way to associate himself with the press release which you have drafted and would have to repudiate it if he were approached on the subject.

As I hope was clear from my letter of 11 February it is unlikely that anything will come of the suggestion you made in your original letter.

With good wishes.

Yours sincerely

+ Thungate

The Most Revd Francis Wagstaffe
3 New Walk
Beverley
EAST RIDING
Yorkshire

Francis Wagstaffe
28 Danesway
Beverley
East Riding
Yorkshire
HU17 7JQ

The Bishop of Birmingham,
Bishop's Palace.
Birmingham.

10th May 1993

Dear Bishop,

I am writing to you as a fellow prelate on a matter of some
intimacy. As Archbishop and Metropolitan of the Old Northern
Catholick Church of the East Riding I recently attended our
European Synod (which included the Old Kalendrists in England,
led by Mar Denis) in Amsterdam. We are not a large body
(though my own is!) and generally meet in some discreet hotel
for a quiet get-together and a bit of sight-seeing.

I happened to be commenting in the bar as to how immaculate
you have always looked, compared to Lord Runcie and Dr. Carey
(but then most bishops do, compared with him, don't they!).
Imagine my surprise when the barman said he knew you very
well. Naturally we all turned our attention to him and he
later vouchsafed in confidence to <u>myself alone</u> and my Vicar-
General, Canon o' Reilley, that this was because you had
access to the facilities of a superb man's corsetiere.

Now, as I flippantly mentioned above, I am not exactly slim
myself (I began to put on weight when I was the non-teaching
proprietor of a prep school - Potter Hall, famous in the East
Riding, where I'm afraid I partook too freely of the
temptations on offer!, and then later as a pork butcher).
There used to be a superb little man in Hull, by the Fish
Dock, who made stays for the fuller male figure, but he had to
close down some years ago!

Could you please share with me the name of the man who does
them for you? I would be verey grateful and not indiscretely
inform anyone else of where I got the information.

Yours sincerely,

+ Francis Wagstaffe

The Most Reverend Francis Wagstaffe - Metropolitan and Primate
- Old Northern Catholick Church of the East Riding.
Order of St. John of Beverley.

Francis Wagstaffe

Garter King at Arms,
College of Heralds.
Queen Victoria Street.
EC4V 4BT

24th May 1993

Dear Garter,

I have recently become the sole proprietor of the Old Northern
Catholick Church of the East Riding, and I am consequently its
Archbishop, Primate and Metropolitan. You will probably have
heard that the Church of England is about to split because it
is going to ordain priestesses. This will mean that a lot of
people will join our church as we will offer proper
traditional worship for ENGLISH people.

The thing is, that our church has now come to the point where
we need orders of distinction like the ones the Archbishop of
Canterbury has, like the Lambeth Cross. You don't need to
worry about the international implications of it won't be like
the Pope putting his detestable enourmities through the door,
and we are ENGLISH!

My honour is the Order of St John of Beverley, with three
divisions:

i) O St. J. of B. First Class (breast star, neck badge, and
sash) Known as Knight Grand Commander.

ii)O St. J. of B. Second Class (neck badge only, and medal)
Known as Grand Commander.

iii) O St. J of B. Thoird Class (medal only) Known as
Commander.

I think we ought to have a Bene Merito Award as well, for
people like cleaning ladies, altar boys, Lord Mayors, etc.
This could be awarded by the Lord Lieutenant.

Up to press, I am the only holder of the Order (First Class),
and my regalia is only worn in private and at our Synods, but
as the church grows with converts from the C of E we will need
to wear them in public.

I have three questions:

a) before I award my nephew, Colin, and his friend Kevin the
2nd Class do I need to register my award with the College of
Arms?

b) do I need a chitty from you before these orders can be worn
in public?

c) do we need some sort of official permission to put 'Sir' on
our cheque books when we get the Knight Grand Commander?

These will have their female equivalents, in the case of the top two - Dame and Grand Dame.

We have no plans, at present for orders of peerage, as follows:

Northern Baronet.

Northern Marquis.

Northern Baron.

Northern Viscount.

Northern Earl.

Northern Duke.

but we would welcome your comments.

All titles, awards and decorations will be in my personal gift and will be kept only for persons of the highest distinction and achievement, not no-hopers like Jimmy Savile, Jimmy Young and David Frost who gain other honours!

I have fixed it with the Lord Chancellor for our bishops to sit in the House of Lords, and I am also in negotiations with Lord (Woy) Jenkins for us to have some Professors in Oxford.

Your early reply would be appreciated. After all, we can't have an Archbishop ending up in the High Court of Chivalry, can we?

Yours sincerely,

+ Francis Wagstaffe

The Most Reverend Francis Wagstaffe - Metropolitan and Primate, Old Northern Catholick Church of the East Riding Order of St. John of Beverley (First class)

From
Conrad Swan, Esquire,
C.V.O., Ph.D., F.S.A.,
Garter Principal King of Arms

College of Arms,
Queen Victoria Street,
London, EC4V, 4BT.,
Telephone: 071. 248. 1188

CS/AMRH

Francis Wagstaffe Esq,
28 Danesway,
Beverley,
East Riding,
Yorkshire,
HU17 7JQ

26 May 1993

Mr. Wagstaffe,

Thank you for your letter of 24 May.

As part of the Royal Household, the College of Arms is only able
to take note of those Knighthoods which emanate from The Crown,
as the Fount of Honour, or those which similarly emanate from
other Sovereign authorities recognised as such by The Crown.

Yours sincerely,

Conrad Swan
Garter.

Francis Wagstaffe

3 New Walk, Beverley, East Riding, Yorkshire

The General Secretary,
General Synod of the Church of England
Church House
Westminster.,
SW1P 3NZ

24th May 1993

Dear Sir,

May I offer you my sympathy for the difficult times your
Church is going through, and extend to you my Archiepiscopal
greetings.

As you may have heard on the grape vine, the Old Northern
Catholick Church is going to be nominated by the Archbishop of
Canterbury as the offical alternative to the C of E in the
North when women are ordained as priestesses in your church.

Until recently, we have been a small body, and have found an
episcopal synod quite enough for our needs. I have been able
to govern through general edict and a series of ad hominem
pastoral letters (some of them more ad hominem than
pastoral!). Now the members are asking for a wider synod to be
formed, to prepare for our sudden growth in numbers. I am not
entirely happy about this, but I think it is probably best to
look as though I am giving in, then to frame standing orders
in such a way that although there is an appearance of decision
sharing all the real power remains with me. What I would
like from you is some tips about how to go about this and how
you do it.

I have decided to appoint my nephew, Colin, as the first
General Secretary, so I would like to come and see you to chat
about it. We have to be in London on business in Great Queen
Street on the 3rd of next month, so we'll pop in, if we may.

I look forward to meeting you.

Yours sincerely,

+ Francis Wagstaffe

The Most Reverend Francis Wagstaffe
Archbishop of the Old Northern Catholick Church
of the East Riding
Metropolitan and Primate
Order of St. John of Beverley (First class)

The General Synod of the Church of England
Church House, Great Smith Street, London SW1P 3NZ Telephone: 071-222 9011
Fax: 071-233 2660

F Wagstaffe Esq
3 New Walk
BEVERLEY
E Yorks

28 May 1993

Dear Mr Wagstaffe

EPISCOPAL SYNOD OF THE OLD NORTHERN CATHOLICK CHURCH

Thank you for your letter of 24 May.

I am afraid that the Secretary-General, Philip Mawer, is otherwise engaged on 3 June, and hence will be unable to meet you and your nephew.

Yours sincerely

C D Ball
Private Secretary
(Dictated personally but signed in his absence)

Francis Wagstaffe
28 Danesway
Beverley
East Riding
Yorkshire
HU17 7JQ

Edward Hughes, esq.
c/o Faber and Faber
3 Quen Square
WC1

Dear Poet Laureate,

May I say what a privilege it is to be writing to you. We are
all very proud of our Yorkshire bard.

I am the sole proprietor of a growning church, and am planning
the opening of our new cathedral (designed by Mr Quinlan
Terry). I've always been fond of verse (Stabber o' Reilley
sometimes has me in tucks with his recitations - but they
wouldn't be entirely suitable for what I have in mind), and I
am commissioning an ode for the ceremony. I thought that Mr
Cyril Fletcher would be the man, but my nephew, Colin, says
not. Mrs Wagstaffe said that we should go straight to the top
and ask the Poet Laureate. The girl in the library was very
helpful (for a change!) and she told us your name and address.
You can imagine our surprise and delight when she said you
were Yorkshire as well.

Colin flew into a rage at this, and it turned out that he
wanted to write the poem all along, so, we've let him have a
go. Could you cast your expert eye over it and let me know
what you think? It seems a bit modern to me. Perhaps you could
make any corrections that you think would improve it. Also
would it read aloud? My neice, Mavis, will be reading it,
standing in for Mrs Wagstaffe, who has broken her teeth.

With thanks and Yorkshire Blessings,

+ Francis Wagstaffe

The Most Reverend Francis Wagstaffe
Archbishop of the Old Northern Catholick Church
of the East Riding
Metropolitan and Primate
Order of St. John of Beverley (First class)

Ode to the East Riding

Skies like Yorkshire slate:
The white rose shivers
And expectation hovers
Like a blade-beaked kestrel.

The future hangs limp –
A whisky-priest,
Flaccid, yet potent.
Dreams writhing at his feet.

Thoughts rise,
Orisons like a ptarmigan's warning.
Awake.
Cut.
Bite.
Inspire.
And yet
In the grounding of the hedgerow's twilight
The vole shrieks.

Francis Wagstaffe
28 Danesway
Beverley
East Riding
Yorkshire
HU17 7JQ

Edward Hughes, esq.
c/o Faber and Faber
3 Queen Square
WC1

13th July 1993

Dear Poet Laureate,

We are just about to go to the printers with the menu for the
banquet, following my enthronement. Colin's poem 'Ode to the
East Riding' will be printed on the card, and we assume that
it will be all right, as you have cast your eye over it, to
say that it come with your 'imprimateur', as we say in the
Church! It just means that you think it's a fine piece of
work. Unless we hear from you by the 20th July (when we 'go to
press') that you think it could be tweaked a little, then
we'll assume we can put your name on the cards. Would you
like to come? We'd be honoured to have you there. Service in
November, banquet following - tickets £50.00p.

With all best wishes and Yorkshire blesssings.

+ Francis Wagstaffe

The Most Reverend Francis Wagstaffe
Archbishop of the Old Northern Catholick Church
of the East Riding
Metropolitan and Primate
Order of St. John of Beverley (First class)

Francis Wagstaffe

3 New Walk, Beverley, East Riding, Yorkshire.

The Right Honorable Lord Jenkins,
House of Lords,
Westminster.

10th May 1993

Dear Lord Jenkins,

Stabber O' Reilly tells me you are Chancellor of Oxford University. I didn't go there myself, but I have been involved in education as the non-teaching proprietor of a Prep School (Potter Hall, famous in the East Riding) so I know how important it is to go to a good establishment, whether you learn anything while you're there or not. The name's what counts. And Oxford is still a good name.

You may have read that the Church of England is going to ordain women as priestesses and that this will split the Church. I have recently become the sole proprietor of the Old Northern Catholick Church of the East Riding, which provides traditional relgiion for English people. I expect a huge influx of members when the C of E finally does the deed. We are getting seats in the House of Lords when the time comes, and will be the official receiving house for defectors up in the North. So, we're a fast growing church!

Where you come in is, my nephew Colin tells me that the C of E has certain jobs in Oxford stitched up, because it is the national Church - professorships and the like. Colin was briefly an undergraduate at Oxford, where his life was changed when he heard a sermon by the famous evangelist and mild arsonist Michael Green, but that's all by the by. Once the split comes, it will no longer be right for the C of E to hold on to all of these top jobs. We would like them allocated on a pro-rata basis, with so many given to us in proportion to the number of people who come over. Can you tell me - how many professors are there in Oxford who have to be C of E? Does the money go with the job, or does the C of E put some up? We don't have a lot of spare capital at the moment, but obviously the Church Commissioners will have to find us some in the near future. I could ear mark some of this for professors if I had to. We could easily recoup such an investment by giving private tuition to dunces. (I believe you were at Balliol, so you know that they keep places back for people with the right connections but who can hardly write their names). Are there any special qualifications, other than being C of E for being a professor of divinity in the University of Oxford?

This is probably all a bit byzantine to you, being Welsh and Chapel, but believe me, it will mean a lot to us, as a growing church to have professors at Oxford.

Yours sincerely,

+ Francis Wagstaffe

The Most Reverend Francis Wagstaffe - Metropolitan and Primate, Old
Northern Catholick Church of the East Riding. Order of St John of
Beverley.

From the Chancellor of the University of Oxford
The Rt. Hon. Lord Jenkins of Hillhead

House of Lords
London SW1A 0PW

19th May 1993

Dear Mr. Wagstaffe,

Thank you for your letter of 10th May. The only Oxford professorships in the category you mention are those which are held jointly with canonries of Christ Church, a college which was founded by Henry VIII and contains the cathedral church of the diocese of Oxford. I doubt if you would find this very promising ground.

Yours sincerely,

Roy Jenkins

The Most Reverend Francis Wagstaffe

Francis Wagstaffe

3 New Walk, Beverley, East Riding, Yorkshire

The Right Honorable Lord Jenkins,
House of Lords.
Westminster.

24th May 1993

Dear Lord Jenkins,

Thank you for your letter of 19th May. It is customary to
address me as Your Grace, as the Archbishop of Canterbury's
Office does, but never mind.

You don't seem quite to have got my drift. It is exactly
<u>because</u> these professors were made by people like Henry VIII
that they can no longer belong to the C of E which has
betrayed its trust. They must be shared out now. What do you
think ought to be my first move in getting some? Should I
write to the Queen saying that you mentioned the Royal
connection? And how many are there? If you don't know perhaps
you could get someone to ask.

You say that they are all at Christ Church. That should make
it easier for us, because it's always been a dunces college,
hasn't it? When Robert Browning found that his son was too
stupid to go to Balliol he sent him to Christ Church, so there
should be plenty of extra coaching there for our professors.

I ought also to mention that there would be a good market for
giving people honorary degrees from Oxford in exchange for,
how shall we say, a consideration. I know this goes on a bit
already and we wouldn't milk the system.

I hope you can help me in this matter.

Yours sincerely,

+ Francis Wagstaffe

The Most Reverend Francis Wagstaffe - Metropolitan and
Primate, Old Northern Catholick Church of the East Riding.
Order of St John of Beverley.

Francis Wagstaffe
28 Danesway
Beverley
East Riding
Yorkshire
HU17 7JQ

Miss Cilla Black,
Blind Date.
LWT
South Bank T.V. Centre
Kent House.
Upper Ground.
SE1 9LT

24th May 1993

Dear Miss Black,

I am writing to you in a professional capacity. Since my
elevation as Archbishop, Primate and Metropolitan in the Old
Northern Catholick Church of the East riding my life has been
transformed — socially as well as ecclesiastically — and Mrs
Wagstaffe and I now attend some of th esmartest Rotary, Round
Tables and Masonics (on Ladies Nights) in the East Riding.

Unfortunately my escort has seriously declined in her physical
attrativeness, recently having suffered from the shock of me
being an Archbishop she had gone completely bald — practically
overnight! Obviously, this puts an intolerable strain on my
standing — not only in the community but in the Church. I
wrote to the Bishop of Oxford, who is also bald, for some help
with hair pieces, but he was dismissive of my approach. Only
last week at our Synod in Amnsterdam I was forced to buy Mrs
Wagstaffe one of those litle flat caps you see Thora Hird
wearing. They don't allow her to take it off either, do they?

In any event, I have decided to 'put her away quietly' —
though of course I can't tell you how!

This leaves me free to find another companion and help-meet in
my life, and I was wondering how to get on your excellent show
'Blind Date'. It must be fairly easy, given some of the
stooges you have on. you must be scraping the barrel. And a
real Archbishop would be a real coup for you, wouldn't it?

Friends and fellow prelates say I have an out-going nature and
even if I don't have the looks of Jason Donovan, at least I'm
taller than the Bishop of Hull (but then who isn't!)

Yours sincerely,

Francis Wagstaffe.

The Most Reverend Francis Wagstaffe — Metropolitan and
Primate, Old Northern Catholick Church of the East Riding.
Order of St. John of Beverley.

Francis Wagstaffe
28 Danesway
Beverley
East Riding
Yorkshire
HU17 7JQ

Miss Cilla Black,
Blind Date.
LWT
South Bank T.V. Centre
Kent House.
Upper Ground.
SE1 9LT

13th July 1993

Dear Cilla (if I may),

I'm sorry to have to pester you, but I wonder if you can let
me have an answer to my letter (I'm putting you a copy in here
in case you've mislaid it!).

It's getting bit urgent, because I've got to make arrangements
for several functions which need a consort (if you get my
drift!), and she's become completely unsuitable.

With best wishes and Yorkshire blesings.

Francis Wagstaffe,

The Most Reverend Francis Wagstaffe
Archbishop of the Old Northern Catholick Church
of the East Riding
Metropolitan and Primate
Order of St. John of Beverley (First class)

COMPLETE AND RETURN
THIS FORM TO
BLIND DATE
LWT
LONDON
SE1 9LT

FULL NAME _FRANCIS WAGSTAFFE_

FULL ADDRESS _28 DANESWAY._
BEVERLEY.
EAST RIDING

TEL NO: INCL.STD CODE

(H)_____ (W)_____

NEAREST MAJOR TOWN: _BEVERLEY_

DO YOU HAVE A PASSPORT? YES/NO _____

IF YES:1 YEAR/10 YEAR _____

DO YOU HAVE A DRIVERS LICENCE?_NO_

DO YOU SMOKE? _____NO_____

PRESENT OCCUPATION _ARCHBISHOP_

AGE _63_ HEIGHT _5ft 3in_

DATE OF BIRTH: _23. 2. 1930_

PLACE OF BIRTH: _BEVERLEY_

MARITAL STATUS: _NEGOTIABLE_

AGE OF CHILDREN: _VARIOUS_

STATE OF HEALTH (PLEASE MENTION
ANY PHYSICAL DISABILITIES:)
EXCELLENT (SOME TROUBLE WITH WATERWORKS)

HAVE YOU APPLIED PREVIOUSLY TO
APPEAR ON BLIND DATE? YES/NO

HAVE YOU EVER APPEARED ON TV?
IF YES GIVE DETAILS
OFTEN IN PROFESSIONAL
CAPACITY.

FOR LWT USE ONLY:										
		G/B	T.O	HOLS	PH	RR	DIS	T/B	V	G

BRIEF DETAILS OF PREVIOUS JOBS/STUDIES _PREP SCHOOL PROPRIETOR. PORK BUTCHER ASTROLOGER. HERBALIST._

WHAT ARE YOUR HOBBIES OR INTERESTS? _PREP SCHOOLS. PORK. ASTROLOGY. REINCARNATION. BALLROOM DANCING. TRAVEL. SPORT(!) THE RAF._

WHAT IS YOUR AMBITION? _TO SHAKE LORD HAILSHAM BY THE HAND_

WHAT TYPE OF MUSIC DO YOU LIKE? _EASY LISTENING (JASON DONOVAN) PROPER HYMNS._

WHERE DO YOU NORMALLY GO ON HOLIDAY? _FILEY. AMSTERDAM_

WHAT IS YOUR BEST QUALITY? _EASY-GOING, YET FIRM_

WHAT IS YOUR WORST QUALITY? _A TENDENCY TO FLATULENCE._

NAME SOMEONE YOU ADMIRE AND SAY WHY _REICHSMARSHALL HERMANN GOERING, FOR HIS DRESS SENSE and HIS DEVOTION TO CULTURE_

WHO WOULD BE YOUR IDEAL BLIND DATE AND WHY? _BARBARA WINSOR JASON DONOVAN, MRS POTTER(ALL BLONDES WITH A SENSE OF FUN.)_

WHAT WOULD BE YOUR IDEAL DAY OUT? _A DAY AT THE RACES WITH A LUCKY COMPANION. OR A TRIP IN A HOT AIR BALLOON WITH A GOOD FRIEND!_

WHY WOULD YOU MAKE A GOOD BLIND DATE CONTESTANT? _I WOULD BRING SOME RESPECTABILITY AND CLASS TO YOUR SHOW._

I UNDERSTAND THAT COMPLETING THIS FORM DOES NOT GUARANTEE ME AN INTERVIEW OR A PLACE ON BLIND DATE

SIGNED...Francis Haughtey.... DATE.15/8/93............

FOR LWT USE ONLY:

Francis Wagstaffe
28 Danesway
Beverley
East Riding
Yorkshire
HU17 7JQ

Watts and Co.
7 Tufton Street,
London.
SW1P 3QE

25th May 1993

Dear Watts,

I am told that you make up clothes for clergymen. As the
Archbishop of The East Riding, I am planning to make some non-
residentiary canons, and I want something proper for them to
wear. They will all be people famous in their own sphere, and
will want the best.

My nephew, Colin, (who was a server in a famous Brighton
church) has designed the cassocks, which are to be orange with
mauve trim and buttons. He says that they will have matching
birettas and over-copes. These are fairly easy to run up, and
his friend, Kevin, is very handy with a needle. The problem
is, Colin says we need almuses (is that how you spell it?) and
that we need you to make them for us. We need a dozen (to
start of with) in silver fox. But if push comes to shove any
colour fox would do.

What would your cost be for these items?

Yours sincerely,

+ Francis Wagstaffe

The Most Reverend Francis Wagstaffe
Archbishop of the Old Northern Catholick Church
of the East Riding
Metropolitan and Primate
Order of St. John of Beverley (First class)

Francis Wagstaffe
28 Danesway
Beverley
East Riding
Yorkshire
HU17 7JQ

The Hon Rocco Forte,
Trust House Forte,
166 High Holborn.
WC1V 6TT

9th June 1993

Dear Rocco Forte,

I wonder if your organization would be able to help us to find
a suitable venue for our General Synod when we meet in August?

We had hoped to be accomodated at an hotel in Scarborough, but
it has just fallen into the sea (this sort of thing seems to
dog our footsteps. Once, when we held our Episcopal Synod at
the Gay Dog Hotel in Amsterdam the fire alarms went off in the
middle of the night. Canon O' Reilley pluckily rescued a
chambermaid, but my nephew Colin twisted his ankle on the fire
escape - he had left his spectacles in his friend Kevin's room
and had been just trying to recover them when the alarm
sounded. Still, all's well....).

We would like somewhere in Harrogate, if you have it. I
normally take a complete floor of luxury rooms for the
prelates, with a suite for myself. You can squeeze the laity
into any sort of annex you like; they will be paying their own
way. We model our structure on that of the Church of England
in these matters. We also need prive sauna and hot tub
facilities - we have a developed theology of leisure.

I know that Billy Butlin lets bishops have his camps at
special rates for conferences for all the clergy, and I
wondered if you could run such a scheme for us?

The hotel would need to have ballroom of suitable size and
grandeur for our services. And you'd better get the staff to
turn off the smoke alarms - Kevin's a glutton for the incense!

I look forward to hearing what terms you have for us.

With good wishes and Yorkshire blessings,

The Most Reverend Francis Wagstaffe
Archbishop of the Old Northern Catholick Church
of the East Riding
Metropolitan and Primate
Order of St. John of Beverley (First class)

FORTE

HOTELS

JD/0693/44

18th June 1993

The Most Reverend Francis Wagstaffe,
28 Danesway,
Beverley,
East Riding,
Yorkshire,
HU17 7JQ.

Your Grace,

Mr. Forte has passed your letter dated 9th June to me in my
capacity as spiritual advisor to our Northern hotels.

I am most concerned to learn of the fate of your 1993 venue,
which clearly had not benefitted from the care and attention
of our new central maintenance team.

I think Harrogate is an inspired choice, although its
residents lack that special warmth you associate with
Amsterdam's. Indeed, it is always cold for the time of year
and when it's not, it's wet! However, your flock could
recuperate with vigorous workouts in our health and leisure
club, where we would be pleased to burn incense whilst the
prelates pumped iron.

For further details of this exciting opportunity, will you
kindly get in touch with the manager, who can be contacted
courtesy of Pannal Golf Club.

In the meantime, may I seek your prayers for our test team at
Headingley and for the selectors' wisdom to select some
Yorkshiremen.

With reverend regards,

Canon Christopher Beaumont
Executive Director

Forte Hotels St. Martin's House 20 Queensmere Slough Berkshire SL1 1YY England
Telephone 0753 573266 Telex 847836 Fax 0753 577227

Forte (UK) Limited Registered in England under number 769170 Registered Office 166 High Holborn London WC1V 6TT

Francis Wagstaffe
28 Danesway
Beverley
East Riding
Yorkshire
HU17 7JQ

The Commanding Officer,
Royal Regiment of Artillery,
17th Training Regiment,
Repository Road,
Woolwich.
SE18 4BB

11th June 193

Dear Sir,

I am making arrangements for my forthcoming Enthronement in
own newly-restored Pro-cathedral, and I wish to know how many
guns I am entitled to for my formal salute upon taking
ceremonial and actual posession of my temporalities. Stabber
O' Reilley tells me that the maximum permissible for one not
of the. royal blood is nineteen. Is this right?

Also, how much do your lads charge for firing them off (their
guns, that is!). I don't want the King's Troop because our
Cathedral is up a cul de sac near the fish dock and there
would be no room for them to turn round. We will of course
provide tea afterwards.

Nearer the time I will send you a map of the area. As I have
said, there is a problem about space, and if you were to set
off the canon in the piazza outside the North door there is
every chance they could blow out the windows in the
Trawlerman's Relief public house opposite, so I think the best
plan is to ask the council to move the tenants out of Herring
Yard for an hour or so to cart the guns down there. After all,
I don't want to be enthroned to the sound of breaking glass,
do I?

With good wishes and Yorkshire blessings,

+ Francis Wagstaffe

The Most Reverend Francis Wagstaffe
Archbishop of the Old Northern Catholick Church
of the East Riding
Metropolitan and Primate
Order of St. John of Beverley (First class)

From: Major M G Tindall Royal Artillery

2IC/DO

17TH TRAINING REGIMENT
ROYAL ARTILLERY AND DEPOT
RA BARRACKS
WOOLWICH
LONDON SE18 4BB
TEL: 081-854-2242 EXT 3251

Francis Wagstaffe Esq
28 Danesway
BEVERLEY
East Riding
Yorkshire
HU17 7JQ

23 June 1993

Dear Mr Wagstaffe,

Thank you for your letter dated 11 June 1993 to the Commanding Officer, he has asked me to reply on his behalf. May I start by offering you the Commanding Officer's congratulations on your imminent Enthronement and his best wishes in the taking possession of your temporalities at what no doubt will be a splendid and memorable ceremony.

To answer your query as to the number of guns to which you might be entitled I have to inform you with regret that despite the importance of the occasion to the Old Northern Catholick Church the event does not qualify for a Gun Salute, although your advice was correct in that a nineteen gun salute is the maximum permitted for those not of royal blood. Stabber O' Reilley may be interested in the relevent extract from The Queen's Regulations:

> para 6.077 states " Salutes other than those authorized by these regulations are not to be allowed, except such as may be necessary for the fulfilment of any treaty obligation, provided that, on any important occasion (eg a great victory gained by Her Majesty's forces) the governor of any of Her Majesty's territories abroad may direct such salutes to be fired as the occasion may seem him to require. Should there be any of Her Majesty's ships present, the decision is to be taken in conjunction with the senior naval officer, and salutes are not to be fired unless the 2 officers concur in the matter."

Following these clear guidelines I have to inform you that a Gun Salute would not be appropriate for the occasion. This will no doubt save great inconvenience to yourselves, the regulars of the Trawlerman's Relief and the tenants of Herring Yard.

An alternative possibility which you may wish to pursue with the Royal Air Force is a Salute in the Air, the format of which is also detailed in The Queen's Regulations:

> para J8.080 states " The approved method of saluting from aircraft consists of a shallow dive and climb, but it is only to be carried out when there is a saluting base on the ground at a display or on special occasions when duly authorized by the commanding officer of the station concerned. The flying restrictions prescribed in Military Flying Regulations (JSP 318) are to be observed."

It would seem that the Royal Air Force is able to exercise a little more flexibility and offers the added advantage of considerably less noise, providing of course that a smallish plane is available for saluting purposes. I feel sure there will be a local Station with suitable aircraft, although may I be so bold to suggest that perhaps a microlight would be more suited than one of the high performance fighters that would be likely to cause not inconsiderable alarm and disturbance to the inhabitants of Beverley and the attendant angels. Whilst not wishing to belittle the ceremony there is also the consideration of cost which inevitably must be borne by yourselves. I am sure, however, that the local Station Commander would be able to advise on the feasibility of such a salute and the type of aircraft best employed.

May I again wish you well for the forthcoming ceremony and the period of your tenure.

Good luck,

Yours Sincerely

Mike Twidam

Francis Wagstaffe
28 Danesway
Beverley
East Riding
Yorkshire
HU17 7JQ

Quinlan Terry

Dear Terry,

I have recently become the sole proprietor of the Old Northern
Catholick Church of the East Riding. There has always been a
lot of potential in religion for people in your line of work,
but now I beleive that it will provide a good opening for
people like myself. I have been in business in a small way for
many years, making a success of a Prep School (Potter Hall,
famous in the East Riding) and a pork butcher's. I burned my
fingers in publishing (Acorn Press), but we are on the right
rails again with the Old Northern Catholick Church.

The reason I am writing to you is that I have managed to pick
up a suitable spot for our new Cathedral. It was a gas pumping
station near the fish dock in Hull, but it has POTENTIAL, and
we would probably get a grant to save it. At our extraordinary
Synod in Amsterdam, the bishops were unanimous that you would
be the man to transform it into something which would be a
worthy place of worship but have all the glitz of the old
Hammersmith Palais de Danse. In other words, exactly the same
job as you did at Brentwood Cathedral which rescued you from
designing those Mercury Telephone Kisks.

The plans would have to include seven thousand green encaustic
tiles, which Mrs Wagstaffe picked up from the demolition sale
at the slipper baths in Sculcoates. She had to get them
because they were a job lot with the sixteen chandeliers which
we also want you to include.

Can you let me know what your estimate for the job would be?

Yours sincerely,

+ Francis Wagstaffe

The Most Reverend Francis Wagstaffe
Archbishop of the Old Northern Catholick Church
of the East Riding.
Metropolitan and Primate
Order of St John of Beverley, (First Class)

Francis Wagstaffe
28 Danesway
Beverley
East Riding
Yorkshire
HU17 7JQ

Brian Hanson,
Church House,
Dean's Yard.
Westminster.
SW1P 3NZ

11th June 1993

Dear Mr Hanson,

We have found ourselve in a bit of a quandry, and wonder if
you could help us out?

Following the demise of Mar Terry the First, who had the only
copy of our Old Dispensations and Formularies, and which he
insisted were interred with him, we are now urgently in need
of a new Code of Canon Law. (My nephew, Colin, suggested we
just take them from him, but I can't face either the prospect
of the legal quibbling which an exhumation order would entail,
or the midnight expedition with shovels).

Our previous regulations were, like the Anglican ones, archaic
and unenforceable, giving me infinite leeway for
interpretation and disciplinary powers, and I can se no reason
to change them, but it is quite an effort getting them re-
written from memory. Are the Canons of the Church of England
copyright, or could we take them, more or less for ourselves,
with just a few alterations?

We wouldn't need to incorporate Canons 1 - 7 inclusive, but
given the problems we have with Mar Walter and his Old
Kalendrists we would like to keep a toe-hold on A8. Apart from
that, other than changing the designation of the Ordinary (in
all cases, my good self) we would only need to tinker with
B30. After Dr Carey made his position clear on the Jimmy
Young Show (which is a novel forum for Ex-Cathedra statements
of doctrine) that there is no need to stay married to someone
if it is inconvenient, I suppose this will be ammended
eventually, but given that only one of our clergy has not been
divorced at least twice I'm afraid we would have to scrub that
one pronto.

Can you advise, please?

With best wishes and Yorkshire blessings,

+Francis Wagstaffe

The Most Reverend Francis Wagstaffe
Archbishop of the Old Northern Catholick Church
of the East Riding
Metropolitan and Primate
Order of St. John of Beverley (First class)

B.J.T. HANSON
Solicitor and Notary

Registrar of the Province
of Canterbury and of York

Registrar of the Convocation
of Canterbury

Church House
Great Smith Street
Westminster SW1P 3NZ
Telephone: 071-222 9011
Fax: 071 233 2660

16 June 1993

The Most Revd Francis Wagstaffe O St J B
28 Danesway
Beverley
East Riding
Yorkshire
HU17 7JQ

Your Grace.

In thanking you for your letter of 11 June we were pained to read of the demise of Mar Terry and even more pained to read that he had taken the Old Dispensations with him. It does seem rather careless and we suggest you should be more vigilant in future.

The Canons of the Church of England are, of course, copyright but, if you will promise to light a candle or two at the Shrine of the Blessed David Johnson, we would be willing to grant dispensation. We take it that the latest changes to the Canons concerning women's ordination will not be tampered with even if this means the Old Northern Catholick Church ordaining ladies.

We were surprised that you wished to retain Canon A 8 (Of Schisms) because no-one has taken any notice of it in the Church of England for decades. The same might also be said of Canon B 30 but perhaps on second thoughts one should say nothing about it. Obviously your Church's policy on this issue would need scrutiny and if you need an independent lawyer to hold an investigation you should consider the writer whose rates are reasonable by comparison with some QC's he could mention.

Yours dutifully

B J T Hanson

B J T Hanson

PS If there is any future correspondence between us would you please note that lawyers are styled Esquire - clergy are the worst offenders in this regard.

PPS Being a Yorkshireman one would quite like to be considered for the order of St John of Beverley (even third class).

Francis Wagstaffe
28 Danesway
Beverley
East Riding
Yorkshire
HU17 7JQ

Sir Brian Hanson,
Church House,
Great Smith Street
Westminster.
SW1P 3NZ

22nd June 1993

Dear Sir Brian

Thank you for your warm and helpful letter. We have set in
train the arrangements for duplicating our ammended version of
the Canons of the C of E. Luckily for us, we won't have to
have lady priestesses, because we accept your kind offer of
free use of them before Parliament ammends the relevant Canon,
so it's full steam ahead. As Canon O' Reiley pointed out,
there would be little hope for the growth of the Old Northern
Catholick Church of the East Riding if we marched in step with
the C of E on that one!

As a Yorkshireman you will have two good reasons to rejoice
this week First, at the reinstatement of the old Ridings,
including our beloved East Riding. This will give a boost to
us! Second, that we have admitted you to the Order of St John
of Beverley (first class). No longer will you need to labour
under the demeaning title of Esquire. So, arise, Sir Brian!

The recipient of the honour usually pays a consideration
towards administrative and secretarial expenses (£50,000.00p -
cheap compared to what the Tories charge), but we will waive
it in your case, and hope that when we accept your offer of
legal advice (which may be quite soon!) you will be similarly
generous.

With congratulations and Yorkshire blessings,

+ Francis Wagstaffe

The Most Reverend Francis Wagstaffe
Archbishop of the Old Northern Catholick Church
of the East Riding
Metropolitan and Primate
Order of St. John of Beverley (First class)

By these Presents

Brian Hanson

has been admitted

Grand Knight Commander

of

the Order of

St. John of Beverley

(first class)

+*Francis Wagstaffe.*

the Most Reverend Francis Wagstaffe

Metropolitan and Primate

The Old Northern Catholick

Church

of the East Riding

Francis Wagstaffe
28 Danesway
Beverley
East Riding
Yorkshire
HU17 7JQ

Mr. Martin Amis,
Peters, Frazer, Dunlop
503 The Chambers.
Chelsea Harbour.
London.

15th June 1993

Dear Mr Amis,

May I say straight away what a fan I am of your work. There
has not been a finer novel in English this century than your
excellent 'Lucky Jim', brought to life so convincingly by Mr
Ian Carmichael.

I can't say that I had seen anything else of yours, until my
nephew, Colin, showed me a copy of 'Money'. What a sad falling
off there has been there. Still, never mind, I am sure you
will regain your form, second novels are often the most
difficult I am told. Keep at it!

I wonder if you feel that you would get more respect from the
general public and from reviewers and the like if you had a
degree? It is always an advantage in a man of letters, as Jim
Dixon knew all too well! As the Archbishop of the Old Northern
Catholick Church of the East Riding, I am, like Dr Carey, in a
position to award degrees from our Episcopal University. These
would have exactly the same academic standing as honorary
Lambeth Degrees. While you will appreciate that they are
absolutley not for sale, they are given at my discretion, and
a donation to our church would make a lot of difference to my
judgement. £250.00. would be the sort of gift a B.A. would
make. M.A.s often feel they would like to offer £500.00p to
our work, while £1,000.00p is an appropriate gift from a
Doctor of Divinity.

I hope soon to be reading reviews of the newest comic novel of
our distinguished man of letters, Dr. Martin Amis.

With all good wishes and Yorkshire blessings,

+ Francis Wagstaffe -

        The Most Reverend Francis Wagstaffe
    Archbishop of the Old Northern Catholick Church
                 of the East Riding
                Metropolitan and Primate
        Order of St. John of Beverley (First class)

Episcopal University

of

The Old Northern Catholick

Church

of the East Riding

Degree

of

Doctor of Divinity

awarded to: *Martin Amis* .

Chancellor

the Most Reverend Francis Wagstaffe

Metropolitan and Primate

Order of St. John of Beverley

(First Class)

Francis Wagstaffe
28 Danesway
Beverley
East Riding
Yorkshire
HU17 7JQ

The Chairman of British Rail,
Euston House,
24 Eversholt Street,
PO Box
100
NW1 1DZ

15th June 1993

Dear Sir,

I see that you are namimg trains after worthwhile causes and
individuals. Only the other week, on 'Praise Be!' Thora Hird
showed us one being named after the 'Girl's Brigade'. Well
done! This is a clear moral lead to our nation.

I hesitate to mention the next bit of my letter, but I am
obliged to do so, by order of our faithful, gathered at an
episcopal colloquium. In a move, entirely unprompted by
myself, they were unamimous in their desire that an engine
should be named the 'Archbishop Wagstaffe Flyer'. This is, as
they put it 'in recognition of the contribution of the work
and influence of our Church in the East Riding'.. No amount of
appeals by me to dissuade them would diminish their fervour in
this, so I reluctantly give in. They have asked me to write to
ask how this may be achieved.

My diary is fairly full over the summer, but I am free in
September to go to York to launch it, and perhaps drive it the
first few miles out of the station.

It would give great pleasure to my nephew, Colin, and his
friend, Kevin, both keen train-spotters, if they could join me
on the footplate (but not to it!)

I look forward to hearing from you.

With all good wishes and Yorkshire blessings,

The Most Reverend Francis Wagstaffe
Archbishop of the Old Northern Catholick Church
of the East Riding
Metropolitan and Primate
Order of St. John of Beverley (First class)

Public Affairs Manager
InterCity 100
Euston House
24 Eversholt Street
London NW1 1DZ

Tel : 071-214 9800
Fax : 071-214 9918

29 June 1993

The Most Reverend Francis Wagstaffe
Archbishop of the Old Northern Catholick Church
28 Danesway
Beverley
East Riding
Yorkshire
HU17 7JQ

Dear Reverend Wagstaffe

Sir Bob Reid has asked me to thank you for your letter of 15 June about locomotive namings and, as the person primarily responsible for these events, to reply on his behalf.

As you can imagine we receive a very large number of requests for namings, the result being that those relatively few which are selected are programmed a long way in advance, generally to coincide with a significant anniversary or celebration. All our InterCity routes (and it is really only InterCity among the passenger business which carries out namings) have full programmes for this year.

My particular difficulty in looking further ahead is that as part of the process of privatisation InterCity fragments into eight independently managed train operating companies from April next year and from this date all our trains pass into the ownership of three leasing companies. How such things as locomotive namings will be taken forward from this time is not yet clear.

For all these reasons I am not able to consider your request for the time being. I hope you will understand my reasons.

Yours sincerely

Brian Daniels
Public Affairs Manager

Francis Wagstaffe
28 Danesway
Beverley
East Riding
Yorkshire
HU17 7JQ

The Minister of Transport,
Ministry of Transport
London.

16th June 1993

Dear Minister,

The Old Northern Catholick Church of the East Riding is
entirely apolitical, and we have no views on the current
transport policy (or lack of it) of the present government.
But there is a matter, near to our hearts, which may be
pertinent to your department and plans.

Do your proposals to privatize British Rail in any way
jeopardize our plans to have a locomtive named after myself? I
do not want to go to all the trouble of launching the
'Archbishop Wagstaffe Flyer' if, in a year's time, Richard
Branson is going to have the whole thing repainted in a vulgar
livery, stocked with French Letter Machines and running day
trips to Whitby, when my faithful anticipate the train
becoming as famous as the Blue Arrow or the Flying Scotchman.

Could you please advise?

With all best wishes and Yorkshire blesings,

+ Francis Wagstaffe

The Most Reverend Francis Wagstaffe
Archbishop of the Old Northern Catholick Church
of the East Riding
Metropolitan and Primate
Order of St. John of Beverley (First class)

147

THE DEPARTMENT
OF TRANSPORT

FROM THE MINISTER FOR PUBLIC TRANSPORT

2 MARSHAM STREET LONDON SW1P 3EB
TELEPHONE 071-276 3000

The Most Reverend Francis Wagstaffe
28 Danesway
BEVERLEY
East Riding
Yorkshire
BU17 7JQ

My Ref: **F/PSO/12974/93**

Your Ref:

6 July 1993

Dear Mr Wagstaffe,

Thank you for your letter of 16 June about the naming of locomotives after the privatisation of the railways.

There is no reason why, following the re-structuring of the railways, that locomotives cannot continue to be named in much the same way as they are now. The difference will be that the locomotives will be owned by 3 rolling stock leasing companies and it will be they, probably in conjunction with the franchisee, who will have a view whether particular locomotives should be named. As is the position now, Ministers will not be in a position to dictate which locomotives carry names, for how long, or in what livery.

Yours sincerely

Roger Freeman

ROGER FREEMAN

Francis Wagstaffe
28 Danesway
Beverley
East Riding
Yorkshire
HU17 7JQ

The Rev'd Alan Dunstan,
c/o Gloucester Cathedral.
Gloucester.

13th July 1993

Dear Rev Dunstan,

I was very interested to read about your life's work as a
hymnologist, and your retirement in the Church Times recently.
Hymns are a great way of getting our message across!

As you can see, from the enclosed letter, the BBC are very
interested in televising one of our services, and I am in
negotiation with them at the moment to cover my imminent
enthronement.

My nephew, Colin, has written a fine hymn, to the tune of
'Polly put the kettle on' (a little naive, I know, but it
needs a simple tune for the faithful to be able to pick up
easily on a first sight). He got the idea from a poem by
George Herbert. The hymn will cover the action of preparing my
regalia on the sedilia. I am ceremonially vested before I am
led to my enthronement, by Canon o'Reilley, the Archimandrite
of Holderness.

Would you kindly run your eye over it, for scansion, logigal
thought and clarity of theological purpose? We will,
naturally, credit you, in the order of service, as our advisor
in this.

With all best wishes for your retirement, and Yorkshire
blessings,

+ Francis Wagstaffe

The Most Reverend Francis Wagstaffe
Archbishop of the Old Northern Catholick Church
of the East Riding
Metropolitan and Primate
Order of St. John of Beverley (First class)

Now our prelate stands alone
Ready now his See to own.
E're he goes to take his throne
He must be dressed

Chirothecae made of suede
And the crozier displayed,
Soon they all will be arrayed
For him to vest.

Buskins made of damask red,
O'er the sanctuary will tread.
Mitre for his Grace's head
With lappets gold.

See the spendid amethyst
Ring for the Archbishop's fist,
By the faithful people kissed
In custom old.

On sedilia we place
Sacred vestments for his Grace
Rochet trimmed with finest lace
And Pallium

Sprinkle them with water clear,
For his fit enthronment here,
Now the time is very near
His hour has come.

7 The Crescent,Truro, Cornwall TR1 3ES

7 College Green, Gloucester GL1 2LX

Canon Alan Dunstan

Telephone (0452) 523987

2o July 1993

The Most Reverend Francis Wagstaffe
28 Danesway,
Beverley,
East Riding
Yorkshire
HU 17 7 JQ

Dear Archbishop,

Thank you for your letter and kind wishes. I am sorry that I do not feel able to comment on the verses which you enclose. They do not seem to me to constitute a Christian hymn, which surely must in some way be in praise of God.

Yours sincerely,

Alan Dunstan

Francis Wagstaffe
28 Danesway
Beverley
East Riding
Yorkshire
HU17 7JQ

The Rev'd Alan Dunstan,
7 The Crescent,
Truro.
Cornwall
TR1 3ES

30th July 1993

Dear Rev Dunstan,

Thank you for your letter and good wishes.

I must say I am a bit flummoxed at what you have to say, and
my nephew, Colin, was very upset at your harsh words about his
hymn. You say you do not feel able to comment on his hymn, and
then you go on to make the most unkind and discouraging
coments I can imagine. We do not understand. As Colin says,
the vestments themselves have mystic meaning and are a way of
praise, so a hymn about them is also a way of praise. I must
agree with him. What do you wear for Matins? A lounge suit? I
think not. So do your splendid robes mean more than adornment?
Enough said, I think.

I told Colin we should leave your name off the order of
service altogether, as you have been so unheplful, but he has
a lovely nature and says we must still mention your name, as
we have written to you and you have bothered to answer, so the
Order of Service will now say: Robing Hymn by Colin Wagstaffe
- Consultant, the Rev Alan Dunstan.

With all best wishes and Yorkshire blessings.

+ Francis Wagstaffe

The Most Reverend Francis Wagstaffe
Archbishop of the Old Northern Catholick Church
of the East Riding
Metropolitan and Primate
Order of St. John of Beverley (First class)

Francis Wagstaffe
28 Danesway
Beverley
East Riding
Yorkshire
HU17 7JQ

Quinlan Terry
Old Exchange,
High Street,
Dedham.
Colchester.
CO7 6HA

Dear Terry,

I am sorry to pester you, but are those designs you promised
me for our new pro-cathedral are ready yet?

As you can see, from the enclosed letter from Ernest Rea, the
BBC are very anxious to broadcast their Christams Eve service
from the cathedral, and it will be good publicity for your
designs, keeping you before the public eye. I know how soon
whizz-kids are forgotten! Look at those seedy gates they've
just put up in London, going nowhere.

I'm glad I've had the chance to buck you up before you
finalise the designs. We need to make sure that the main west
doors will be big enough to take a full-grown camel (laden).
We're having a beast our church sponsors from London Zoo for
the opening ceremony - 'Camels that bear spices and gold in
abundance, and precious stones' (2 Chronicles, chapter 9 verse
1). I hope you'll be there as well, to present your building.

With all good wishes and Yorkshire blessings.

Francis Wagstaffe

The Most Reverend Francis Wagstaffe
Archbishop of the Old Northern Catholick Church
of the East Riding.
Metropolitan and Primate
Order of St John of Beverley, (First Class)

Francis Wagstaffe
28 Danesway
Beverley
East Riding
Yorkshire
HU17 7JQ

Alan Yentob,
BBC
Broadcasting House.
London.
W1A 1AA
14th June 1993

Dear Mr Yentob,

We are beginning to make our preparations for Christmas, as I suppose you are, too.

You must have noticed the unsavory tendency of the BBC to climax its Christmas religious broadcasting with a midnight service from a C of E or RC church. Now, I read in the Daily Telegraph that you intend to shake up 'Auntie's' image, and I hope that this will include breaking up this religious cartel. Indeed, I would suggest that you need look no further than yours truly.

By December I should have been formally enthroned in my new Cathedral, refurbished by Quinlan Terry. The liturgy, worked out by my nephew, Colin's friend, Kevin, (who studied under the late Sir Frederick Ashyton and Fr Desmond Morse-Boycott) has variously been described as 'exquisite', 'beyond compare' and 'a treat' (the last by Mrs Wagstaffe, who has an eye). Kevin also designed the vestments, based on patterns held at Santiago de Compostella. These have been embroidered by my neice, Mavis, and are the envy of Humberside. Our honorary canons who are in attendance at major festivals, gloriously arrayed in choir in habits unique to ourselves, with silver fur almuses made by a Royal Warrant Holder! So, as you can see, a midnight eucharist from the Old Northern Catholick Church of the East Riding will be a visual delight.

Our services are in the common tongue, and would be very easy for your viewers to follow (if they can understand Brian Glover they can follow us!) But our displaced epiclesis might require your commentator to provide an explanatory comment (which I will be happy to provide).

I understand that a facility fee is generally claimed for outside broadcasts of this nature, and I would be happy, under the circumstances, to settle for £5,000. cash.

With all best wishes and Yorkshire blessings,

✝ *Francis Wagstaffe*

The Most Reverend Francis Wagstaffe
Archbishop of the Old Northern Catholick Church
of the East Riding
Metropolitan and Primate
Order of St. John of Beverley (First class)

NORTH

BRITISH BROADCASTING CORPORATION
NEW BROADCASTING HOUSE
PO BOX 27
OXFORD ROAD
MANCHESTER M60 1SJ
TELEPHONE: 061-200 2020
TELEX: 265781 BBC HQG PASS TO MRA
FAX: 061-236 1005

5th July 1993

Dear Archbishop,

Alan Yentob has sent me your letter and asked me to reply. Responsibility for the scheduling of our Church Services on BBC Television resides with me. In fact we frequently broadcast from non conformist churches on Christmas Eve, although their practice of having midnight celebrations is not as common as with Anglicans and Roman Catholics.

We have already chosen the venue for 1993 as these things require detailed planning. I will ask one of my colleagues to pay a visit to your Church. In the meantime it would be helpful if you could give me details of the frequency of your services, the numbers regularly attending, and the quality of your musical resources.

I am afraid that you have high expectations of the facility fee paid by the BBC on such occasions. Should we broadcast from your Church we would pay a mere fraction of the amount you suggest.

Yours sincerely,

(Ernest Rea)
Head of Religious Broadcasting

The Most Reverend Francis Wagstaffe
28 Danesway
Beverley
East Riding
Yorkshire   HU17 7JQ

Francis Wagstaffe
28 Danesway
Beverley
East Riding
Yorkshire
HU17 7JQ

Air Commodore M Barnes,
Director, RAF Public Relations
Ministry of Defence.
London

13th July 1993

Dear Air Commodore,

I am writing to you, at the suggestion of Major M. G. Tindall,
Royal Artillery, who says that you would be able to provide us
with a salute in the air, on the occasion of my enthronement
in our new pro-cathedral in Hull. He explains that such an
event would be less hazardous to the area than a gun-salute,
and he refers me to Queen's Regulations, para J8.080. I am
sure you are familiar with this.

Please could you tell me how to proceed, how many aircraft you
intend to use, and what types?

Would it be possible for my nephew, Colin, to be in the
cockpit of one of the planes? He has always awanted to fly,
and he could get some good aerial snaps of the ceremony from
that vantage point.

With all good wishes and Yorkshire blessings.

+ Francis Wagstaffe

The Most Reverend Francis Wagstaffe
Archbishop of the Old Northern Catholick Church
of the East Riding
Metropolitan and Primate
Order of St. John of Beverley (First class)

From: Air Commodore B E A Pegnall, Director of Public Relations
(RAF).

MINISTRY OF DEFENCE
Main Building, Whitehall, London SW1A 2HB
Telephone (Direct Dialling) 071-21-8
(Switchboard) 071-21-89000
7905

D/DPR/330/1

The Most Reverend Francis Wagstaffe
28 Danesway
Beverley
East Riding
Yorkshire HU17 7JQ

21 July 1993

Your Grace,

    I am replying to your letter to Air Commodore Barnes of 13
July. Please be advised that Mike Barnes left the RAF some two
years ago, hence my response.

    I fear that the allocation of RAF aircraft for formal
flypasts is not within my gift. However, I have passed your
letter to Mr Chris Kingham, who is Secretary of our Participation
Committee at Strike Command, High Wycombe. It is that body which
has executive responsibility for requests such as yours. I have
asked Chris to reply to you directly, but it would be useful to
know the date of your enthronement, since your note makes no
mention of it.

    With every good wish for a successful outcome.

Yours sincerely,

Brian Pegnall

Recycled Paper

From Ms Susan Alexander,
RAF Participation Committee Secretariat
Room 148, B Block

Headquarters Strike Command

Royal Air Force High Wycombe Buckinghamshire HP14 4UE

Telephone: High Wycombe (STD 0494) 461461 Ext 7441

F Wagstaffe Esq
28 Danesway
Beverley
East Riding
Yorkshire   HU17 7JQ

Reference
STC/90386/2/93

27 July 1993

Dear Sir

REQUEST FOR RAF FLYPAST

Thank you for your letter of 13 July to the Director of RAF
Public Relations which has been passed to me for reply.

I regret the RAF will be unable to provide a flypast as
outlined in your letter. I am sure you will appreciate that
we receive many hundreds of similar requests each year, but to
support them all would divert manpower and resources from
their primary tasks.

I am sorry to have to send a disappointing reply.

Yours sincerely

S. Alexander

Francis Wagstaffe
28 Danesway
Beverley
East Riding
Yorkshire
HU17 7JQ

Ms Susan Alexander,
RAF Participation Committee Secretariat,
Room 148
B Block.
Headquarters Strike Command
RAF
High Wycombe
Bucks.
HP14 4UE

30th July 1993

Dear Susan,

I am writing to you about your very curious letter of the 27th
July. I wonder if I may take you to task on a few points?

You say that you 'receive many hundreds of similar requests
each year'. Really? Enthronments of Archbishops in their new
Pro-cathedrals? Hundreds? Please could you list the ten most
recent for me? Then you say that it would 'divert manpower and
resources from their primary tasks'. What primary tasks?

I do not wish to seem to stand on my dignity, but may I also
remind you that Air Commodore B.E.A. Bagnall addresses me as
'The Most Reverend' and greets me 'Your Grace' as is proper,
not 'Esq' and 'Sir'. You may wish to be Ms, but please
remember the dignity due to others.

I wish to be kind, and my nephew, Colin points out that you
may have taken more on yourself than you should. So, I shall
not write back to the Air Commodore or to Mr Kingham reporting
your laspe of judgement. Up here, in the East Riding, we have
rather old fashioned views on what things the ladies are
capable of, and organising fly pasts is not amongst them. I
look forward to your early reply assuring me of your co
operation.

With all good wishes and Yorkshire blessings.

The Most Reverend Francis Wagstaffe
Archbishop of the Old Northern Catholick Church
of the East Riding

From: C M Kingham, Secretary, RAF Participation Committee,
Room 148, B Block

Headquarters Strike Command
Royal Air Force High Wycombe Buckinghamshire HP14 4UE
Telephone: High Wycombe (STD 0494) 461461 Ext   7479

Francis Wagstaffe Esq
28 Danesway
Beverley
East Riding
Yorkshire
HU17 7JQ   5 August 1993

Dear Mr Wagstaffe,

Thank you for your letter of 30 July to Susan Alexander
about your request for an RAF flypast. You mentioned that you
were not planning to write to me personally, but, in view of some
of your comments, I feel bound to respond.

You are, of course, quite correct to assume that we do not
receive hundreds of requests for flypasts at enthronement
ceremonies for Archbishops of any denomination; but we do receive
many hundreds of requests for RAF flypasts (and displays) at a
wide variety of events each year (the majority of which we are
regrettably forced to turn down), and it was to this aspect of
our work that Susan drew the similarity to your letter.

The primary roles of the United Kingdom's Armed Forces are
detailed in the annual Statement of the Defence Estimates. In
short, they are: to ensure the protection and security of the
United Kingdom and our dependent territories (even where there
is no major external threat); to insure against any major
external threat to the United Kingdom and our allies; and to
contribute to promoting the United Kingdom's wider security
interests through the maintenance of international peace and
stability.

As you can imagine, flying displays and flypasts are very
much a secondary aim in that context, but they do play an
important role in promoting the image of the RAF in a positive
light, in demonstrating the skills and capabilities of our crews
and equipment in an entertaining way, and in encouraging
potential recruits to consider a career with the Service.
Unfortunately, our display resources are, of necessity, limited,
and we therefore seek to obtain the maximum benefit and public
exposure from every event in which the RAF participates. It is,
however, our policy not to provide flypasts or displays for
private individuals.

With all this in mind, we have tried to determine your own position in the Church (and thereby the likely level of public interest in your enthronement ceremony), but without success. The Beverley Tourist Information Office has researched for us the history of Catholicism in the Kingston-upon-Hull area back to its roots in the 18th Century and can find no trace of the Old Northern Catholick Church of the East Riding Metropolitan or the Order of St John of Beverley. Similarly, our RAF Chaplains are not aware of that church or order; nor is the Deputy Chaplain-General (Army), who recently completed a tour at a unit very close to Beverley. In addition, Hull Council has confirmed that they have received no planning applications for any new cathedrals. Unfortunately, as your letters do not contain a telephone number, and you are not listed with Directory Enquiries, we have been unable to contact you directly to discuss your request.

In these circumstances, therefore, I am entirely satisfied with our original decision not to provide a flypast at your enthronement ceremony. Equally, you will understand our difficulty in referring to you as "The Most Reverend" or "Your Grace", without formal confirmation that you are a properly appointed Anglican or Old Dutch Catholic Archbishop, or Roman Catholic Bishop.

I would not wish to comment in detail on your opinions of women in general, except to say that they are not ones which I share. However, Susan is - despite your views - more than capable of arranging the odd flypast. In fact, she almost single-handedly manages the RAF's annual participation programme, which is a substantial task, requiring a high degree of political acumen and organisational skill. You may also be interested to know that she is held in very high regard by all her colleagues within the RAF, as well as by the many display organisers and other members of the public with whom she comes into contact during the course of her work.

I am sorry to have to send you another disappointing reply about the flypast, but I hope I have been able to clarify the other points you raised. I am copying this letter, and yours, to Air Commodore Pegnall (to whom you wrote initially with your request); he will no doubt be interested in this exchange of correspondence.

Yours sincerely

CM Kingham

Francis Wagstaffe
28 Danesway
Beverley
East Riding
Yorkshire
HU17 7JQ

C. M. Kingham,
RAF Participation Committee Secretariat,
Room 148
B Block.
Headquarters Strike Command
RAF
High Wycombe
Bucks.
HP14 4UE

10th August 1993

Dear Chris,

I am a bit flummoxed about your letter of August 5th, but I am willing to
give you the benefit of the doubt, as you are a civilian working in a
service situation which may perhaps puzzle you by its complexity.

I must take you to task on the matter of my designation. I can assure you
that in all my dealings with Lambeth Palace I am addressed as 'Your Grace'.
I must also point out that I have had correspondence with Garter King of
Arms about the order of St. John of Beverley, a distinction which he finds
perfectly unexeptionable. It might interest you to know that a very senior
official in Church House Westminster is Sir Brian Hanson, O St. J of B.
(first class)

As to the planning permission for the development work to our cathdedral. I
am at least grateful to you for bringing this to my attention. I had
expected that the distinguished architect, Mr Quinlan Terry, who is under
our instructions, would have had this matter in hand by now, and I will
certainly be contacting him about it.

Please forgive me for pointing out that if you believe that the history of
the Catholick Church in the East Riding has 'its roots in the 18th Century'
you will believe anything! Even the youngsters in our White Army of St
Hilda know better than that!

Now that you have had time to reflect on your oversights I wonder if you
could tell me what sort of aircraft we could expect for our salute in the
air? We would prefer props, rather than jets for two reasons. Canon o'
Reilley has many happy memories of the old kites, and there will be a camel
in the enthronement procession, so I dread the consequences if it is
frightened by a sonic boom.

With all best wishes and Yorkshire blessings.

+ Francis Wagstaffe

The Most Reverend Francis Wagstaffe
Archbishop of the Old Northern Catholick Church
of the East Riding
Metropolitan and Primate
Order of St. John of Beverley (First class)

From: C M Kingham, Secretary, RAF Participation Committee,
Room 148, B Block,

Headquarters Strike Command
Royal Air Force High Wycombe Buckinghamshire HP14 4UE
Telephone: High Wycombe (STD 0494) 461461 Ext 7479

STC/90386/2/93/670

Francis Wagstaffe Esq
28 Danesway
Beverley
East Riding
Yorkshire
HU17 7JQ

16 August 1993

Dear Mr Wagstaffe,

Thank you for your letter of 10 August. I am afraid I have nothing further to add to my letter of 5 August, in that the RAF will not be providing a flypast over your enthronement ceremony.

I am sorry to have to send yet another disappointing reply.

Yours sincerely

C M Kingham

Francis Wagstaffe
28 Danesway
Beverley
East Riding
Yorkshire
HU17 7JQ

The Managing Director,
Madame Tussaud's,
Baker Street.
London.

12th July 1993

Dear Sir,

I was recently embarrassed at our Synod in Amsterdam, to have
to explain to many delegates, Archbishops and Metropolitans
why it was that they had come away disapointed from your
exhibition of waxworks. They had expected to see my effigy
alongside those of other leading Prelates of England.

I naturally brushed aside the grievance, by informing those
from Third World countries especially, that while to them I
might be the best known English clergyman (after the likes of
Lord Soper and the Archdeacon of York), in the UK I was simply
one of many telegenic ecclesiastical dignitaries.

However, as our church is soon to grow both in numbers and in
national profile when we become the official receiving body
for those leaving the Church of England following the
priestess heresy, it might be worth your while preparing an
effigy of me now. (I enclose a Press Release I have prepared
in consultation with Lambeth Palace).

I am coming to town in a couple of weeks time, and will drop
in on the Thursday afternoon to talk about arrangements and
perhaps make a first 'sitting' with your modellers. (about
3.30. if that would suit).

Do I have to loan you the robes, or do you see to all that?

With all best wishes and Yorkshire blessings,

The Most Reverend Francis Wagstaffe
Archbishop of the Old Northern Catholick Church
of the East Riding
Metropolitan and Primate
Order of St. John of Beverley (First class)

MADAME TUSSAUD'S

16th July 1993

Francis Wagstaffe
28 Danesway
Beverley
East Riding
Yorkshire HU17 7JQ

Marylebone Road
London NW1 5LR

Telephone: 071-935 6861
Facsimile: 071-465 0862

Dear Francis Wagstaffe

Thank you for your letter of 12th July to our managing director.
I am afraid we are unable to accept your kind offer to sit for
us.

We portray several world famous religious leaders such as the
Pope and Archbishop Desmond Tutu and at present we do not plan
to add any new figures to this particular group.

We will, however, contact you should we ever decide to include
your likeness in our collection.

Thank you again for your interesting proposal.

Yours sincerely

Juliet Simpkins
Head of Press & Publicity

An attraction in
The Tussauds Group Limited

Registered No. 215035 in London
Registered Office: York Court,
Allsop Place, London NW1 5LR

"Tomaculum"
28 Danesway
Beverley
East Yorkshire
HU17 7JQ

The Ambassador,
Embassy of the Russian Federation.
13 Kensington Palace Gardens.
LONDON
W8 4QX

25th January 1994

Your Excellency,

May I offer you Northern Greetings and Yorkshire Blessings on Holy Mother
russia.

We were delighted to hear that DNA testing has proved beyond doubt that you
have recovered the body of the dear lost Tsar. In our Church he is a martyr
for the faith and his Feast Day falls between S. Gildas the Wise and S.
Reparata.

I am pleased to be able to enclose with this letter one of our most
treasured objects, the ulna of St John of Beverley. We have most of the
rest of his skeleton as well, so we can spare it. In return, we would
appreciate it if you would send us a bone of similar size and quality
belonging to his late Majesty. We would keep it in a specially made
reliquary, which we will commission from Garrards. And we will expose it
annually for the veneration of the Faithful.

Please, do not try to fob us off with a relic of the Princess Anastasia. A
representative of your country tried to do this during the godless days of
communism, and we were not taken in! I know I can tell you in confidence
that the Princess first struck land at Whitby, after her escape, and she
has been a member of our church for many years.

Yours,

+ Francis Wagstaffe

The Most Reverend Francis Wagstaffe
Archbishop of The Old Northern Catholick Church of the East Riding
Metropolitan and Primate
Knight Grand Commander, Order of St. John of Beverley

Embassy of the Russian Federation

13 Kensington Palace Gardens, London W8 4QX

Mr Francis Wagstaffe
"Tomaculum"
28 Danesway, Beverley
East Yorkshire
HU17 7JQ

28 January 1994

Dear Mr Wagstaffe,

Since there is no interest in the exchange proposed
by you. We are obliged to return to you the relic you
treasure so much,

Yours sincerely,

Information Officer

"Tomaculum"
28 Danesway
Beverley
East Yorkshire
HU17 7JQ

Mrs Stella Rimington.
MI5
P.O.Box 3255
London.
SW1P 1AE

9th February 1994

Dear Madam,

I am writing to alert you of the presence of a Bolshevik, acting under
cover as an Information Officer at the Embassy of the Republic of the
Russian Federation. As you can see from the enclosed correspondence, he
scribbles his name, but he should be quite easy to identify. Would you
please tell me what action you intend to take?

I expect there are a lot of the Old Guard lurking about. We still have
trouble with the Old Kalendrists. My Chief of Staff, Canon O' Reilley,
found one posing as a catechumen only the other week!

I wonder if it is worth your while having a look at Canon Michael Green, of
7 The Green, Chilwell, Nottinghsam. NG9 5BE. He is a well known arsonist
and Evangelist He uses Lambeth Palace notepaper, even though he lives in
Nottingham, and he was for a while involved in activity with students at
Oxford, even though the colleges had their own chaplains.

With all best wishes and Yorkshire Blessings.

Yours,

+ Francis Wagstaffe

The Most Reverend Francis Wagstaffe
Archbishop of The Old Northern Catholick Church of the East Riding
Metropolitan and Primate
Knight Grand Commander, Order of St. John of Beverley

PO BOX 3255
LONDON
SW1P 1AE

Rev F Wagstaffe   17th February 1994
"Tomaculum"
28 Danesway
Beverley
East Yorkshire
HU17 7JQ

Dear Reverend Wagstaffe

Thank you for your letter dated 9th February 1994 the contents of
which have been noted.

May I take this opportunity to thank you for your interest in the
Service.

Yours sincerely,

C Sumner
for the Director General

"Tomaculum"
28 Danesway
Beverley
East Yorkshire
HU17 7JQ

The Ambassador,
Embassy of the Russian Federation.
13 Kensington Palace Gardens.
LONDON
W8 4QX

8th February 1994

Your Excellency,

I am sorry to have to report a very serious matter to you. I enclose a
letter I sent on 25th January, and which I am sure has never reached you.

Your so-called Information Officer, who scribbles his name, so I can not
identify him, has intercepted a most valuable relic, and has returned it.

The man is clearly a Bolshevik, and is a danger to you. No true mujik would
deal in such a way with a pious matter. He must be rooted out and dealt
with. I am sure there are many of them still hanging round waiting to come
back to power. They never will!
I return our precious relic, and await your attention.

As a matter of State Security I am copying this correspondence to Stella
Rimmington, as I know you now work openly hand in glove with our spy
network, not, as your predecessors did, under cover.

With all best wishes and Yorkshire Blessings.

Yours,

+ Francis Wagstaffe

The Most Reverend Francis Wagstaffe
Archbishop of The Old Northern Catholick Church of the East Riding
Metropolitan and Primate
Knight Grand Commander, Order of St. John of Beverley

Embassy of the Russian Federation

13 Kensington Palace Gardens, London W8 4QX

Mr Francis Wagstaffe
"Tomaculum"
28 Danesway
Beverley
East Yorkshire
HU17 7JQ

14 February 1994

Dear Mr Wagstaffe,

Confirming that there is no interest displayed in the exchange proposed by you we are obliged to again return to you the relic you treasure so much and ask you not to send it to us any more.

You may though try and contact the Russian church authorities to seek their advice on the idea developed by you.

Yours sincerely,

Vladimir Molchanov
First Secretary

Francis Wagstaffe
28 Danesway
Beverley
East Riding
Yorkshire
HU17 7JQ

Ernest Rea,
BBC
New Broadcasting House,
PO Box 27
Oxford Road.
Manchester
M60 1SJ

13th July 1993

Dear Mr Rea,

Thank you for your letter. I think you're very wise to take up our offer,
but that you will kick yourself if you wait until 1994. By then you'll have
missed the boat on the great celebrations for the re-establishment of the
East Riding.

Perhaps you would like to consider the service for my enthronemnt and the
dedication of our new pro-cathedral in November of this year?

In answer to your questions.

At the present we are a little strapped for space, while waiting for the
work to be completed on our new building. We have a solemn liturgy every
Sunday at 5.30.pm. The numbers depend on the time of year, importnace of
the occasion, and rigorousness of the preparatory period of fasting. There
is also the matter of the attendance at the Prothesis, which clutters up
things a little. So, as you can see, it is hard for me to give you an
honest and unvariable number. But, let me assure you, we are well-
supported, and will grow rapidly when the C of E ordains priestesses. And,
as you know, the attraction of the cameras boosts the congregation. I've
seen Songs of Priase come from packed churchess, which normally count
themselves lucky to have three old ladies and a parrot.

We are very proud of our music. The liturgy is entirely sung, to mozarabic
chant, with intrumental accompaniment provided by members of the White Army
of Saint Hilda (our youth organisation). We do not have clapping, humming,
bajoes, or kazoos!

I look forward to doing business with you. A mere fraction of £5,000 will
be all right with us. As long as it's a big fraction!

With good wishes and Yorkshire blessings.

The Most Reverend Francis Wagstaffe
Archbishop of the Old Northern Catholick Church
of the East Riding
Metropolitan and Primate
Order of St. John of Beverley (First class)

N O R T H

BRITISH BROADCASTING CORPORATION
NEW BROADCASTING HOUSE
PO BOX 27
OXFORD ROAD
MANCHESTER M60 1SJ
TELEPHONE: 061-200 2020
TELEX: 265781 BBC HQG PASS TO MRA
FAX: 061-236 1005

20th July 1993

Dear Archbishop,

I do not want to mislead you. What I wrote in my original letter was that I would ask someone from my department to visit your Church and investigate its potential for broadcast. I can give no undertaking beyond that, and I certainly think it unlikely that we would be asking you to broadcast within the next 12 months.

With best wishes.

Yours sincerely,

Jacqueline A. Mahony

(Ernest Rea)
Head of Religious Broadcasting

(dictated by Ernest Rea and signed in his absence by his secretary)

The Most Reverend Francis Wagstaffe,
28 Danesway,
BEVERLEY,
East Riding,
Yorkshire,
HU17 7JQ

N O R T H

BRITISH BROADCASTING CORPORATION
NEW BROADCASTING HOUSE
PO BOX 27
OXFORD ROAD
MANCHESTER M60 1SJ
TELEPHONE: 061-200 2020
TELEX: 265781 BBC HQG PASS TO MRA
FAX: 061-236 1005

27th July 1993

Dear Archbishop,

Your letter to Mr. Rea has been passed to me as the person responsible for worship. As you can imagine I am intrigued at the voyage of discovery offered by the prospect of the enthronement of the new Archbishop of the Old Northern Catholic Church of the East Riding. Please forgive my ignorance in that I am not able to glean from your two letters whether the occasion to which you are inviting us is the establishment of a new diocese or just the dedication of a new Archbishop and a new pro-cathedral within the already existing diocese. I have to confess that if it is the latter I was not familiar with your predecessor.

I should be very interested to discover the form that the 'Prothesis' takes and if you could send me a copy of your service book it would be a great help in assessing how, if at all, we can use your liturgy as the basis for a broadcast. I am also intrigued with your reference to the 'Deferred Epiclesis'. This is a new concept to me and I am wondering if it is based on some patristic theology which I have not yet heard of. I look forward to hearing about the liturgical significance of the 'deferral'. As I am sure you are aware the ASB liturgy currently in use in the Anglican Church has restored the use of the Epiclesis but in its accustomed place as in the Liturgy of St. Chrysostom.

There are two matters of fact which I must take up with you. The first is your assertion that churches fill up automatically for the benefit of cameras - they don't. The reason that churches are full for *Songs of Praise* is that they are almost invariably set up as ecumenical occasions inviting church people from the surrounding district. Without a wide spread invitation you might be glad of a resident parrot or a visiting pigeon as long as they can sing in tune. The other factor you cite as a potential booster for your congregation will not really be active at the time for which your enthronement is arranged as the General Synod does not meet to put final touches to the Ordination of Women Measure until November so it would be unwise to assume much movement into the ONCC will have taken place.

May I finish by saying that I look forward to hearing from you and possibly to meeting at some future stage. I do hope you won't be put off by my questions and there is just one more - is the allegiance of the Old Northern Catholic Church of the East Riding more strongly towards the East Riding or to the Old Catholic Church who do not appear to be familiar with your august body?

With best wishes.

Yours sincerely,

(Noel Vincent)
Chief Assistant to the Head of Religious Broadcasting

"Tomaculum"
28 Danesway
Beverley
East Yorkshire
HU17 7JQ

Noel Vincent,
BBC
New Broadcasting House,
PO Box 27
Oxford Road.
Manchester
M60 1SJ

10th August 1993

Dear Mr Vincent,

Thank you for your letter of 27th July. I am delighted that
you are going to broadcast from our new cathedral. You seem to
have forgotten to include the contract with your letter.
Please could you rectify this as soon as possible. I
appreciate that it probably isn't your fault. The girls who
type things up are notoriously slack!

I'm surprised that someone in your position should have such a
loose grip of liturgical terms! I must confess, I am little
shaky myself, but then, with my experience as a prep schol
proprietor I am better informed on the educational and
catechetical side of our life. Our liturgical expert, to whom
I have referred for the answers to your questions, whould have
written to you himself, but he is back in the clinic, with a
recurrence of His Old Trouble! Still, I'll do my best to make
sense of his notes on the subject. I hope you appreciate the
trouble this has taken. My nephew, Colin had to hold his hand
steady as he wrote.

The Prothesis takes the form of stabbing a small loaf of bread
with a boat hook. This combines the symbolism of the ancient
church with the seagoing interests of the East Riding.

The Epiclesis is not deferred, as you maintain, but displaced,
as I said in my first letter. Even a dunce like I am knows you
couldn't defer it! According to Canon o' Reilley, we have an
ealry epiclesis, as they do in the Syrian Liturgy of SS Addai
and Mari, because there is not a full account of the
instituion narrative in the canon. Do you follow?

Now to matters more my speciality!

I'm extremely glad to see that you write that the
congregations for Songs of Praise are bused in from
neighbouring churches! That's obvious to anyone when you see
the tired and haggard faces of those aged crones who've
travelled miles in charabancs over rough terrain, and missed
their afternoon nap and a cup of tea, just to be seen on the

small screen! Nor do I imagine that a simple ecumenical
impulse could have produced half the House of Commons in St.
Margaret's Westminster, when on a good day in St Stephen's
Chapel (without the cameras) you would be lucky to muster Paul
Boetang, Gillian Widdicomb and the Earl of Lauderdale.

As to the November synod meeting. A full church for the
cameras will give our recruiting campaign a great boost! What
do you say?

I'm not surprised that the Old Catholics pretend not to know
about us. We haven't been on terms since Mar Terry fell out
with the Old Kalendrists, and when he died and had the
Dispensations buried with him that was the end of the road!

I look forward to seeing you and your contract.

With good wishes and Yorkshire blessings.

The Most Reverend Francis Wagstaffe
Archbishop of the Old Northern Catholick Church
of the East Riding
Metropolitan and Primate
Order of St. John of Beverley (First class)

"Tomaculum"
28 Danesway
Beverley
East Yorkshire
HU17 7JQ

RSPCA
Causeway.
Horsham.
West Sussex.
RH12 1HG

25th January 1994

Dear sir,

Here in the East Riding we are proud of our European connexions, and we always hold our Episcopal Synod in the Low Countries, where life is more relaxed and society more tolerant.

With the coming of the European Union we are keen to extend our horizons and give a more southern European flavour to our summer festivities this year. On Midsummers Day we shall be holding our Summer fete, and we would like to drop a donkey from the tower of Beverley Minster. This would be a great draw for tourists and would givre a touch pf Spanish Magic to our event.

The problem is the spiral stone staircase. The donkey jibs at climbing it.

As you can appreciate, we would not want the donkey to suffer, and my Chief of Staff, Canon O' Reilley, has researched the matter, from the writings of the late Albert Pierpoint. He tells me that the weight of the donkey, the size of the drop, and a small amount of sedative wil be enough to render the beast unconscious before it strikes the ground, so it will feel no pain. But when we ran a trial go (without the drop) the donkey got half way up and would not budge. we had drugged it with some of Mrs Wagstaffe's home made wine to encourage it up the stairs, and there was a bit of a mess afterwards. No harm was done (to the donkey at least, though Canon O' Reilley got a nasty kick in the cassock). Our problem is how to administer the soothing potion at the foot of the stairs without fuddling the donkey, rather than at the top.

Can you please advise and attend?

With all best wishes and Yorkshire Blessings,

Yours

✝ *Francis Wagstaffe*

The Most Reverend Francis Wagstaffe
Archbishop of The Old Northern Catholick Church of the East Riding
Metropolitan and Primate
Knight Grand Commander, Order of St. John of Beverley

"Tomaculum"
28 Danesway
Beverley
East Yorkshire
HU17 7JQ

The Secretary-General,
Churches Together in England.
Inter-Church House.
35-41 Lower Marsh.
London.
SE1 7RL

Monday, March 28, 1994

Reverend and Dear Sir,

I am writing to you in my capacity as Metroplitan and Primate of the Old Northern Catholick Church of the East Riding, to apply for my denomination to join Churches Together. I realise we are only a small (yet rapidly growing) church, but Leroy, the brother of the girl who works in the library, belongs to the Church of the Cherubim and Seraphim, and he told her that you welcome new churches, so you should surely be not averse to admitting one of the older ones like ourselves.

You don't have to tell me that a sad and confused history is liable to make the big denominations wary of bodies labelling themselves Old Catholick (believe me ,we've had troubles with the Old Kalendrists ourselves!) so I feel it it would be only proper and prudent to inform you of our credentials.

We derive our Orders from the Vilatte Connection. As I'm sure you are no doubt aware, Joseph Rene Vilatte (Mar Timotheos I) was raised to the episcopate as the first Old Catholic Archbishop of North America by a Bull of His Holiness Peter III (Jacobite Patriarch of Antioch) by Mar Julius I of the Independent Church of Ceylon, assisted by the Bishops of Kottayam and Niranam in 1892. This Syrian-Malabar succession was secured for our church with the raising of Henry Marsh-Edwards as Bishop of Caerleon by Mar Timotheos in 1903. By this act, in so far as Marsh-Edwards was an Anglican clergyman at the time, the Old Catholic Church in England abandoned its Monophysite associations and adhered, as it does to this day, to the doctrines of Chalcedon. In 1909 Mar Henry raised Henry Bernard Vaughan to the episcopate as Bishop of Dorchester. When Mar Henry II abandoned us to seek Anglican orders from Bishop Winnington-Ingram in 1924 it could have spelt the end of our Brave Little Church, but I am happy to say that before he reneged on us he consecrated Albert Kitchener Bickerdike, of Thorngumbald, as Archbishop of the East Riding in 1922, from whom I, via his son, Mar Terry I, achieve my orders as Mar Francis II. I trust that this makes things clear.

It is true that there have been dissentions in the past. This was initially because at the time of the consecration of Mar Henry I there was already another Bishop of Caerleon, Charles Isaac Stevens (Mar Theophilus I), although he belonged to the Ancient British Church, and since his death as Perpetual Coadjutor in 1916 there have been a number of almost scandalous claims and counter-claims about rights and jurisdictions, but I need not bore you with the details. I am sure you know that Old Kalendrists sow themselves like dragons' teeth. Suffice it to say that their leader is currently Mar Keith II and <u>I strongly advise you to have nothing to do with him!</u>

On a more positive note, we are a thriving church with a splendid new pro-cathedral in progress, and a vibrant youth organization. In addition to reaping the benefits of a wider ecclesial fellowship I also sincerely believe that we could bring a distinct contribution to your body.

I look forward to receiving an application form.

With all good wishes and Yorkshire Blessings.

✠ Francis Wagstaffe

The Most Reverend Francis Wagstaffe
Metropolitan and Primate - The Old Northern Catholick Church of the East Riding
Knight Grand Commander, Order of St. John of Beverley

CHURCHES TOGETHER IN ENGLAND

General Secretary:
The Revd Canon Martin Reardon
Inter Church House
35-41 Lower Marsh
London SE1 7RL
Tel: 071-620 4444
Fax: 071-928 5771

Registered Charity Number 1005368

Field Officer (North & Midlands)
Mrs Jenny Carpenter
Crookes Valley Methodist Church
Crookesmoor Road
Sheffield S6 3FQ
Tel: 0742 682151

Please reply to:
London

Field Officer (South)
The Revd Roger Nunn
Baptist House
129 Broadway, Didcot
Oxon OX11 8XD
Tel: 0235 511622

8 April 1994

The Most Rev. Francis Wagstaffe
Tomaculum
28 Danesway
Beverley
East Yorkshire
HU17 7JQ

Dear Archbishop Francis

Thank you for your letter of 28 March.

I enclose a copy of our Constitution which includes our Basis and fundamental requirement for Membership.

Normally we admit into membership at the <u>national</u> level only Churches which have at least 2000 members in England spread in at least 10 local congregations. We believe that normally that is necessary if Churches are to play their full part as members at national level. If they are not of this size, they are, of course, free to approach their local Council of Churches or Churches Together for admission to membership at local level, and the decision on membership will be made by the Churches already in membership at that level.

If you wish to pursue the possibility of membership with us, perhaps you would kindly let me have details of your doctrinal basis, number of members and churches in England etc, and I will put your request initially to our membership committee.

With all good wishes.

Yours sincerely

Martin Reardon

(The Rev. Canon) Martin Reardon
General Secretary

Enc

Francis Wagstaffe
28 Danesway
Beverley
East Riding
Yorkshire
HU17 7JQ

The Director,
Victoria and Albert Museum.
Brompton road.
Kensington.
London.

13th July 1993

Dear Sir,

Sadly, Mar Terry, our Primate, died recently, and I have
become his successor. In going through his documents and
files, I have discovered a receipt from your museum, for the
Maniple of St John of Beverley, which we lent to you, for six
months in 1971, for a special exhibition.   Mar Terry, though
a good man, was not an able administrator, and it seems that
he never recovered the sacred item, and that it is still with
you.

I wonder if you could let me know how much you owe us, for the
extra time you have had the maniple? I also think it would be
a good thing if I could pop down and have a poke around in
your drawers to see if there are any other things which he
may, in misplaced kindness, have let you borrow without a
receipt. We are, for instance, still unable to locate the
following items, which were in our last inventory but are now
missing:

a) left buskin of Cardinal Pole (green damask - cross keys)
b) pome, (silver) engraved with pelican
c) two lappets (mitre missing) gold thread with Peter and Paul
d) reliquary - (legend -' membrum Sancti Ceaddae virile')
e) liturgical comb (ivory - double-sided, carved with biblical
   scenes)
f) Archbishop Wolsey's chirothecae. Red with strapwork.

I hope you can help us to revover some of these items, and
that you will return the maniple as soon as possible. I should
like to wear it at my enthronement in November.

With good wishes and Yorkshire blessings.

The Most Reverend Francis Wagstaffe
Archbishop of the Old Northern Catholick Church
of the East Riding
Metropolitan and Primate
Order of St. John of Beverley (First class)

The Most Reverend Francis Wagstaffe
Archbishop of
The Old Northern Catholic Church of East Riding
28 Danesway
Beverley
EAST RIDING
Yorkshire
HU17 7JQ

27 July 1993

Dear Sir,

The Director has asked me to thank you very much for your letter which, as it relates to ecclesiastical textiles, she has forwarded to me for reply.

I apologise for the slight delay in contacting you but I have been away from the Museum at a conference.

It would aid us enormously if you could possibly forward a photocopy of the receipt you mention. This will speed the search through our extremely thorough records. With the information available we have been unable to locate records of the maniple. The other objects which you list are not in the Museum. The major exhibition here in 1971 was devoted solely to Victorian Church Art; it excited a great deal of interest at the time and saw a marked increase in visitors bringing ecclesiastical textiles of all periods and description to the V&A for identification. A marvellous catalogue accompanied the exhibition and all loans were meticulously recorded and returned to owners afterwards.

Our entire holdings (loans accepted by the Museum as well as objects belonging to the V&A) are catalogued and computerised. Names are crucial to our record searching and we were wondering if Mar Terry dealt with the Museum under his sacerdotal or secular name. This is probably recorded on the receipt and I very much look forward to receiving a copy which should enable us to resolve the question.

Yours sincerely

Valerie D Mendes

Valerie D Mendes
Curator
Textiles and Dress

Victoria and Albert Museum South Kensington London SW7 2RL Telephone 071-938 8500 Telex 268831 VICART G Facsimile 071-938 8458

"Tomaculum"
28 Danesway
Beverley
East Yorkshire
HU17 7JQ

Valerie D Mendes,
Curator,
Textiles and Dress
Victoria and Albert Museum.
South Kensington.
London.
SW7 2RL

25th January 1994

Dear Valerie,

Thank you for your letter of 2nd July 1993, which I must admit flummoxed
me. I am sorry that it has taken me so long to reply, but it has not been
easy for me to put my hands on the documents you asked for. Between you and
me, we are not on good terms with the Old Kalendrists, and that did not
help. I am pleased to say that I am now in a position to furnish you with
them. This is due to the diligence of our Archivist, Canon O' Reilley, and
the good fortune of my nephew, Colin.

You were quite right to spot that the receipt was in Mar Terry's name
before he was raised to the Apostolate. I am enclosing the item, and as you
can see, it is entered under his given name of Athenagorus Bickerdyke. I
hope that this clears up the problem of locating the maniple.

As to the other items. I can find no receipts for any of them, I am afraid.
But this is where our stroke of good luck came in. Colin asked at the
library about the collection, and was surprised to find that the new girl
behind the desk was both knowledgeable and helpful (she won't last long in
the Libraries and Museums service!). She located our ivory comb I mentioned
and which you said you had not got in a book called 'A History of
Ecclesiastical Dress' by Janet Mayo. It was published by Batsford in 1984,
and it may be in your local library if you want to check it up. Meanwhile,
I have got a photocopy that the girl did for Colin for you to look at. The
book makes it quite clear that you have got this item which is very
precious to us. I am amazed you said you had not got it.

We are most anxious to recover both the comb and the maniple as soon as
possible, so could you please send the comb back straight away, and let me
know how you are getting on finding the maniple.

I must say, it is quite a shock for me to find that you do not know what
you have got knocking about in odd corners. May I prevail upon you to allow
me to pay you a visit with our Archivist and with Colin to see what we can
find. We will be in London the first week in February. Shall we call then?

With all best wishes and Yorkshire Blessings,

Yours.

enc: receipt for maniple
     photcopies from 'History of Ecclesiastical Dress'.

The Most Reverend Francis Wagstaffe
Archbishop of The Old Northern Catholick Church of the East Riding
Metropolitan and Primate
Knight Grand Commander, Order of St. John of Beverley

at Lewes in Sussex, where a priory was founded in 1077. Being a reformed order of Benedictines, the Cluniacs retained the black dress.

Colet (also Collet)   A shortened form of acolyte (q.v.). It is not clear whether the loss of the 'a' was due to aphesis or to mistaking it for the indefinite article – a-collyt.

Collare   A richly ornamented collar or tippet, which was sometimes placed over the upper part of the chasuble. It was also known as 'the Flower' (D. Rock, *Church of Our Fathers*, 3 vols, 1849–52).

Colours, Liturgical   Although all vestments were originally plain and white, coloured fabrics

77   This ivory comb, carved with scenes from the Bible, was kept in the church specifically for use by the priest after he had fully vested, as almost all liturgical vestments are put on over the head.

and embroideries were soon introduced. By the twelth century the following colours had been established:

Black: Masses for the dead; Good Friday (silver not gold trim).

White/gold: Christmas and Easter; Epiphany.

Red: apostles; martyr saints (except female virgins); Pentecost.

Violet: Lent; Advent; Rogation days.

Green: Trinity; less traditional, but serves as the all purpose colour.

Blue: no liturgical significance but very popular colour especially in the fourteenth- and fifteenth-century inventories and found in Old Sarum Rite; associated with churches named for Mary.

White: Feast of Virgin Mary; virgin saints.

It would appear, however, that it was not until the end of the nineteenth century in England that these colours were taken too seriously; individual

31 January 1994

The Most Reverend Francis Wagstaffe
Archbishop of the Old Northern Catholik Church of the East Riding
Tomaculum
28 Danesway
BEVERLEY
East Yorkshire
HU17 7JQ

Dear Sir

Thank you for your letter of 25 January which has been passed to me
by Mrs Mendes so that I can explain what we are doing: when we
wrote to you last summer we were concerning ourselves only with
textile items which might relate to our Collection and we apologise
if our failure to consider non-textile items has caused you any
anxiety.

We realise now that the breadth of your enquiry necessitates
detailed liaison among several Departments within the Museum and so
we have passed all our correspondence to The Registrar's Office
within the V&A. They are the one central section with the
resources to sort out everything with speed and efficiency.

Unfortunately, the copy of Mar Terry's receipt for the maniple (in
1971) was not included in your letter of 25 January; I think it
would help The Registrar's Office if you could send it to them.

Yours faithfully

Jennifer Wearden
Deputy Curator
Textiles & Dress Collection

Victoria and Albert Museum South Kensington London SW7 2RL Telephone 071-938 8500 Facsimile 071-938 8458 A charity exempt from registration

The Most Reverend Francis Wagstaffe
Archbishop of the Old Northern Catholick Church of East Riding
28 Danesway
Beverley
East Yorkshire HU17 7JQ

7 February 1994

Dear Sir

Further to Jennifer Wearden's letter to you of 31 January, I am
writing to ask whether you could forward the copy of the receipt
for the maniple which was not enclosed in your letter to her.

Perhaps you could also let me know when the other items you mention
went missing from your inventory, and whether you have any
photographs of them?

Meanwhile, I can confirm that the liturgical comb of which you sent
an illustration is indeed in this Museum. It is on display in our
Mediaeval Treasury, and its Museum Number is A27-1977. Its
provenance is well-recorded, as you will see from the attached
photocopy. I fear it cannot be the one which you have mislaid.

I look forward to hearing from you soon.

Yours sincerely

Hilary Bracegirdle
Registrar

Victoria and Albert Museum South Kensington London SW7 2RL Telephone 071-938 8500 Facsimile 071-938 8458 A charity exempt from registration

CARD 2.

A.27-1977

See David Park, "A New Interpretation of the Magi Scene on a Romanesque Ivory Comb", The British Archaeological Association, cxxxiv, 1981, 29-30.

LENT TO EXHIBITION

Title ENGLISH ROMANESQUE ART , 1066-1200

Dates 5 April - 8 July ,1984

Places Hayward Gallery, London

Catalogue No. 197

Valuation

Weight (if applicable)

R.P.

197 Liturgical comb
Ivory; h 85 mm, w 115 mm
c. 1120; St Albans
London, Victoria and Albert Museum, A.27-1977

The comb is in excellent condition, with only a number of the smaller teeth broken. It shows on one side the Nativity, the Flight into Egypt, the Washing of the Feet of the Disciples, the Last Supper, the Betrayal, the Crucifixion and the Entombment; on the other side are the Massacre of the Innocents, the Adoration of the Magi, the Dream of the Magi and the Annunciation to the Shepherds. The ends of the comb show a continuation of the Annunciation to the Shepherds and the Soldiers on guard at the Sepulchre. The rather stiff figures – often in profile – and the crowded compositions are closely comparable to the illuminations in the St Albans Psalter (17), which is datable to c. 1120-30. P.W.

PROVENANCE Collection of Mrs T.L. Barwick-Baker (Hardwicke Court, Gloucestershire) before 1861; Miss Olive Lloyd-Baker, who placed it on loan to the Victoria and Albert Museum; accepted in lieu of capital transfer tax 1977
EXHIBITIONS Barcelona, 1961, no. 961; London, 1974, no. 18, repr.
BIBLIOGRAPHY Beckwith, 1972, no 61, ills. 128, 129 (with hibliog.); Lasko, 1972a, p. 215; Tcherikover, 1979, pp. 7–21; Park, 1981, pp. 29–30; Williamson, 1982, p. 37, pl. 19

'The Medieval Treasury' (V&A Cat. 1986) pp 110-111

"Tomaculum"
28 Danesway
Beverley
East Yorkshire
HU17 7JQ

The Director,
Victoria and Albert Museum.
South Kensington.
London.
SW7 2RL

19th February 1994

Dear Sir,

I wrote to you last year, in an effort to recover our property and you
passed the matter on to a Valerie Mendes. She denied all knowledge of our
comb, and asked for a receipt for the maniple.

By a stroke of luck I found that your collection does have a comb exactly
like the one she denied. When I drew this to her attention she passed the
letter to an assistant, who has in turn passed it to someone else. And I am
now told that they can not find the receipt I sent!

Now let me make it quite clear that I do not accuse anyone of dishonesty.
but when you deny having things that are in your catalogue, and then you
lose receipts, it makes me wonder whether the place is being run
efficiently.

My Chief of Staff, Canon O' Reilley is muttering about being pipped at the
post to these items by the Old Kalendrists, and that you've given them back
to the wrong people! But I say he's just scare-mongering. We have the same
problems with the girls in our local libraries and museums service. It will
all turn right in the end. But can I please ask you to give this your
urgent personal attention.

I feel I ought to advise you that a casual approach to Holy Things brinngs
its own reward! It did not go unnoticed among the Faithful that when Mar
Timothy II denied that he had got our gremial veil Driffield Cottage
Hospital immediately and unaccountably postponed his operation and he
remained in considerable discomfort for many months!

✝ Francis Wagstaffe

The Most Reverend Francis Wagstaffe
Archbishop of The Old Northern Catholick Church of the East Riding
Metropolitan and Primate
Knight Grand Commander, Order of St. John of Beverley

18 March 1994

Office of the Director

The Most Reverend Francis Wagstaffe
Tomaculum
28 Danesway
Beverley
East Yorkshire HU17 7JQ

Dear Sir,

I am writing in reply to your letter dated 19th February and your earlier correspondence.

We have now checked our records very carefully and I have to inform you that we have no record of any of your objects entering the Museum, either for the 1971 Church Art Exhibition or subsequently. I am afraid that without a copy of the receipt (which was omitted from your letter to Valerie Mendes dated 25th January) we are unable to pursue the matter further.

Yours sincerely,

Elizabeth Esteve-Coll

DIRECTOR

from Elizabeth A L Esteve-Coll

Victoria and Albert Museum South Kensington London SW7 2RL Telephone 071-938 8501/8504 Telex 268831 VICART G Facsimile 071-938 8477

"Tomaculum"
28 Danesway
Beverley
East Yorkshire
HU17 7JQ

The Secretary,
Society for Psychical Research.
49 Marloes Road.
London.
W8 6LA

25th January 1994

Dear Sir, I am writing to you about a very disturbing incident which has come about during the excavations for the ambulatory of our new Pro-cathedral.

My nephew Colin's friend, Kevin, who was told by a gipsy at Stow horse Fair that he is a natural sensitive was recently casually cruising round our building site late at night when he suddenly felt unnaturally cold. He at first thought that this was due to a draught from an unglazed window in the clerestory. But no matter where he moved he found that it followed him round "like a policeman". He did not say anything to me at first, but the next night he spent the night there with a friend, a master mariner who is naturally very level-headed and used to the lonely watches of the night. They became so frightened that they were found huddled together when the workmen arrived the following morning.

Kevin has since discovered from the girl in the library that the area upon which the workmen are digging is reputedly the resting place of pirates hanged and buried without the benefit of the Church's rites.

I have asked an Anglican parson who tells me that it is very dangerous for the inexperienced to attempt an excorcism (in fact he told me of an Archdeacon who bungled one so badly that he had to spend the rest of his ministry in the Church in Wales!).

Is it possible for a member of your Society to investigate this matter and advise me what to do?

With all best wishes and Yorkshire Blessings,

Yours.

The Most Reverend Francis Wagstaffe
Archbishop of The Old Northern Catholick Church of the East Riding
Metropolitan and Primate
Knight Grand Commander, Order of St. John of Beverley

The Incorporated
Society for Psychical Research
ESTABLISHED 1882

Registered Office

Telephone:
01-937 8984
071

49, MARLOES ROAD,
KENSINGTON,
LONDON W8 6LA

31.1.94

The Most Reverend F Wagstaffe
28 Danesway
Beverley
East Yorkshire
HU17 7JQ.

Dear Reverend Wagstaffe,

Thank you for your letter of 25.1.94 which I have
passed to our member Canon M C Perry of Durham whom
we think may be the best person to advise in this
matter.

Yours sincerely,

J W Stiles

J W Stiles

A Company Limited by Guarantee   *Registered No. 44861 C England*

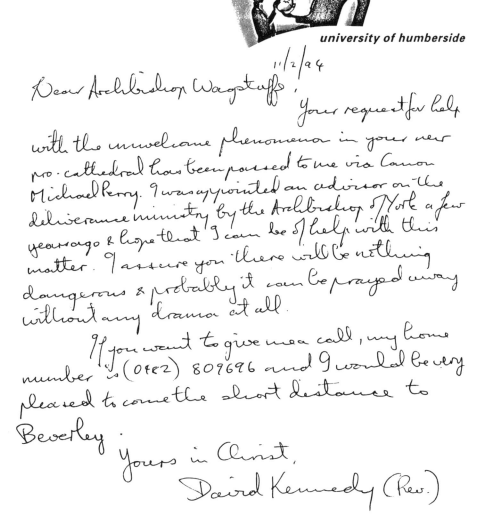

university of humberside

11/2/94

Dear Archbishop Wagstaff,

Your request for help with the unwelcome phenomena in your new pro-cathedral has been passed to me via Canon Michael Perry. I was appointed an advisor on the deliverance ministry by the Archbishop of York a few years ago & hope that I can be of help with this matter. I assure you there will be nothing dangerous & probably it can be prayed away without any drama at all.

If you want to give me a call, my home number is (0482) 809696 and I would be very pleased to come the short distance to Beverley.

Yours in Christ,

David Kennedy (Rev.)

ecumenical chaplaincy

250 Cottingham Road Hull HU6 7RT
Tel 0482 440550 Fax 0482 471342 Telex 592717 HumcolG
Professor R P King Vice Chancellor

Francis Wagstaffe
28 Danesway
Beverley
East Riding
Yorkshire
HU17 7JQ

The Senior Editor,
SCM Press,
26-30 Tottenham Court Road,
London N1 4BZ

10th May 1993

Dear Sir,

I am writing to see if I can interest you in a proposal for a book - 'The
Spiritual Quest of Francis Wagstaffe'.

I have knocked around a bit and seen some of the world, not like a lot of
the parsons who have done books for you in the past. I even ran a small
publishing house of my own once, Acorn Press, you've probably heard of it.
But I think my new idea requires a broader canvas, a national publisher.

What it is, is, I have always been able to take the mood of the public,
meet it, and make a few bob. I ran a Prep School - Potter Hall, famous in
the East Riding, then I snak the profits in a pork butcher's when I was
forced to sell up because of ugly and quite false rumours. So you can see
that I've led a worldly life, but I've thrashed around looking for a code
to live by. I tried a new alphabet for dyslexics, astrology,
reincarnation, herbalism, and they all fell short of what I needed. Then,
pushed in the right direction by a bishop in the Midlands (who I will name
in the book) I took instruction from another bishop and from a famous bald
evangelist and mild arsonist (who I will also name in the book, but not
now!).

The upshot was, when a local church came on hard times (The Old Northern
Catholick Church of the East Riding), I snapped it up, and am now its sole
proprietor and chief man. We are expecting many recruits when the Church
of England ordains priestesses. There is a lot of future in religion. My
Spiritual Quest is the arresting story of a Group Scout Leader who finds
The Way! Your readers will snap it up, and all our members will buy a
copy.

We kan orlso print it in mi nyoo sistum so that dislexix kan reed it
simpli. A seenyer bishup ov the Church ov Ingland hoo iz dislexic wil
recumend it tu yu I am shoor.

Yours sincerely,

+ *Francis Wagstaffe*

The Most Reverend Francis Wagstaffe - Metropolitan and Primate, Old
Northern Catholick Church of the East Riding. Order of St John of
Beverley.

SCM PRESS LTD
26-30 TOTTENHAM ROAD LONDON N1 4BZ
Telephone: 071-249 7262/5 · Fax: 071-249 3776

MEL/JW   26 May 1993

Most Revd Francis Wagstaffe
28 Danesway
Beverley
East Riding
Yorks
HU17 7JQ

Dear Metropolitan

THE SPIRITUAL QUEST OF FRANCIS WAGSTAFFE

Thank you for writing with your proposal for a book.
I am afraid, however, that personal memoirs are not
our area - we specialise in academic theology.   I
am sorry not to be be able to help.

Yours sincerely

pp Jennifer Ellis

Miss M Lydamore
Associate Editor

Francis Wagstaffe
28 Danesway
Beverley
East Riding
Yorkshire
HU17 7JQ

The Religious Books Manager,
Hodder and Stoughton,
Mill Road,
Dunton Green,
Sevenoaks,
Kent.
TN13 2YA

23rd April 1993

Dear Sir/Madam,

I am writing to see if you would be interested in publishing a book of the reminiscences and thoughts of an ordinary man in the street, on the state of Church life today. This is a very important time in the life of the Church, what with an imcompetent as Archbishop of Canterbury, and the poor lead given by the rest of the bishops. I know that many bishops believe in astrology, herbalism, reincarnation and wigs.

I had thought that I would not be able to produce a long enough book, but I have been encouraged to write to you by seeing the work of the famous evangelist and mild arsonist Michael Green. You published his book - WHY BOTHER WITH JESUS? An odd title from a clergyman, I think. But it is only 55 pages long, and I am sure I could do better than that.

My book would be called - WHY BOTHER WITH THE BISHOPS OF THE CHURCH OF ENGLAND? It would be a combination of my thoughts on life, after a full life as a Group Scout Leader, and interviews with bishops. I can get the interviews easily enough because my friend Stabber O' Reilly has a brother-in-law who meets most of them at their lodges. This is the time to get them to speak unguardedly, when they have got one trouser leg rolled up, a left breast exposed and are holding on to the reins of the goat. I can tell you, some of the things that Stabber tells me would make your hair curl, and they would certainly sell books.

I think we have had enough books by parson. Let's have one from the ordinary Group Scout Leader.

Yours sincerely,

+ Francis Wagstaffe

Hodder & Stoughton *Publishers*

47, Bedford Square,
London WC1B 3DP
Telephone: 071-636 9851
Telex: 885887
Fax: 071-631 5248

05/05/93

Mr Francis Wagstaffe
28 Danesway
Beverley
East Riding
Yorkshire
HU17 7JQ

Dear Mr Wagstaffe

Further to your letter of 23rd April, I have now had a chance to take a careful look at
your proposal.

I read this with interest, but I am afraid that the material is not entirely suitable for
our list, and we will not, therefore, be able to take your proposal any further.

I am sorry to disappoint you in this way, but thank you, nonetheless, for sharing your
ideas with us.

With my best wishes,

Yours sincerely

Mrs Bryony Benier
Editorial Assistant
Religious Books

A division of Hodder & Stoughton Limited   Registered Office: Mill Road, Dunton Green, Sevenoaks, Kent   Company No 651692 England

St. Peter's House Young Homeless Support Centre

The charity is based in the heart of the Highfields area of inner-city Leicester. It is home to nineteen homeless men and women aged between sixteen and twenty-five, for as long as it takes them to get back into something approaching a settled existence... and continues to offer support after they have left the House.

St. Peter's is always desperately short of funds to carry on its work, and welcomes donations of cash, goods and services.

St. Peter's House Young Homeless Support Centre,
2, St. Peter's Road, Leicester
LE2 1DA   0533 755298

Registered Charity no. 1020070

Index